Why **Christians** Should **Support Israel**

D1550467

Published by TimeWorthy Books
PO Box 30000
Phoenix, AZ 85046-0009

Printed in the United States of America.

ISBN 0-935199-50-0

Why Christians Should Support Israel

MIKE EVANS

Why **Christians** Should **Support Israel**

srael. By all measures it's a tiny country. With a population of less than 8 million and a land mass that is comparable to the state of New Jersey—the fifth smallest state in the U.S.—Israel's role on the world stage should be relatively minor. Yet, hardly a day goes by when Israel and the Israeli-Palestinian Peace Process do not dominate the international headlines.

Israel has always been surrounded by enemies. On the day after Israel was reborn as an independent nation on May 14, 1948, she was attacked by her much larger Arab neighbors, who supported the Palestinians. Only through the grace and protection of God was Israel able to survive. Again and again over the years this tiny island of freedom has suffered assaults and attacks from evil men dedicated to her destruction.

Today Israel is more isolated than ever before. Security is a constant struggle as all of Israel's neighbors either actively oppose her or at least harbor those who do. Since the reuniting of the city of Jerusalem, there have been nearly 10,000 terrorist attacks in the Bible land. There have been more suicide bombings in the city of Jerusalem than in any city in the world.

As my good friend of more than 30 years, Prime Minister Benjamin Netanyahu has repeatedly pointed out, the issue of contention is not about a Palestinian state, the division of Jerusalem, settlements, checkpoints, security fences, or borders. The issue is Israel's very right to exist as a nation. Most of the Arab world still refuses to accept this simple proposition.

Not only do they think Israel has no right to exist as a _state_, but they think the Jewish _people_ have no right to survive. The resistance of the Arab countries to Israel's national aspirations has always been tied to the Muslim world's ultimate resistance to the right of the Jewish people to exist at all. Peaceful co-existence has never been the goal of the Arabs, nor even having Jews living dispersed in other lands without a country. The real goal has been the abnegation, and in its worst and most absolute form, the very extermination, of the Jewish race itself.

This is why Palestinian children are taught to hate and kill Jews from their first breath and why the Islamic world throws parties in the streets every time Jewish blood is shed. This is why in radical Islamic theology the successful homicidal maiming and murder of Jews represents the highest aspiration many Palestinian mothers have for their children.

Anti-Israeli sentiment has in fact become the new anti-Semitism. It makes Israel the new "collective Jew" which justifies assault on individual Jews as the extension of the state. This hatred—not any other issue—is the true source of murder and terrorism.

Yet amazingly enough, most of the world views tiny, democratic Israel as the threat to peace rather than the homicidal terror-loving powers that surround her.

The friendship between America and Israel has been of the utmost importance to a succession of presidents since Harry Truman who first endorsed the new nation. But in recent years, nations like America and England that have long stood with Israel have moved away from their traditional support. We do so at our own peril because we are standing at a prophetic crossroads—one that will determine the future of our world. We must not fail to do our part to fight and win the battle for Israel's survival.

I speak at conferences and churches across America, and the one question I am constantly asked is, "why should I support Israel—what does Israel have to do with me, with America?" My friend, Israel has everything to do with you, with your family, with your country. The short answer to why you should support Israel is that by blessing Israel, you will be blessed:

"Now the LORD had said to Abram: 'Get out of your country, From your family And from your father's house, To a land that I will show you. I will make you a great nation; I will bless you And make your name great; And you shall be a blessing. I will bless those who bless you, And I will curse him who curses you; And in you all the families of the earth shall be blessed'" (Genesis 12:1-3).

As a Bible-believing Christian, you should support Israel simply because your God ordains it.

But I've written this book for those of you who want the long answer. I've been standing for Israel as your ambassador for decades. I've faced down terrorists and world leaders alike in support of the Jewish people. I don't believe there is a minister of the Gospel who has spoken out on Israel's behalf more than me, and these are my top ten reasons why you, too, should support Israel.

1. Because God Says **He Will Bless Those Who Bless Israel** and Curse Those Who Curse Israel

(Genesis 12:3).

"The LORD shall bless thee out of Zion: and thou shalt see the good of Jerusalem all the days of thy life" (Psalm 128:5, KJV).

irst, let's explore the idea of your blessing or cursing being tied to your treatment of Israel by taking a look back at some recent history.

I stood in shocked silence, and looked into the eyes of our U.S. President at the Madrid Peace Conference. President George H. W. Bush opened the conference at the end of the Persian Gulf War (Spain 1991). Israel was not allowed to join the coalition because all the anti-Semitic Arab countries were screaming. Our President also asked Israel not to retaliate when it was bombarded with 38 SCUD missile attacks, and they honored his request. At the end of the war they were rewarded with a $10 billion dollar loan guarantee freeze. This money was needed to provide housing for refugees, mostly Russian Jews. The enemies of Israel were appeased again when Israel was hauled to Madrid to give up land for peace—peace that has never come. Syria alone was given one billion dollars by the U.S. It was spent on the purchase of North Korean missiles to be used against Israel. Many of those missiles are in Lebanon in the hands of Hezbollah, a Palestinian terrorist organization. The missiles are aimed at the cities of Israel.

THE PERFECT STORM

As President George H. W. Bush was opening the conference at the Royal Palace in Madrid, the Perfect Storm (the one made famous in the movie) developed in the north Atlantic creating the largest waves ever recorded in that region. The storm traveled 1,000 miles "east to west" (as opposed to the normal west to east pattern) to crash into the eastern coast of the United States; smashing 35 foot waves into the Kennebunkport, Maine home of President Bush. This was one of the worst storms in American history and one of the top ten in insurance claims. When the Madrid Conference was moved to Washington, D.C., for a resumption of the land-for-peace talks, Hurricane Andrew struck Florida. It wreaked havoc; causing an estimated $30 billion in damages, leaving 180,000 Americans homeless, and securing a spot on the top ten list of the largest disasters in American history.

"but the people who know their God shall be strong, and carry out great exploits"
(Daniel 11:32).

Every nation in history that has lifted a hand against Israel has been cursed. And every nation that has blessed Israel has been blessed. *"...For he who touches you touches the apple (pupil) of his eye"* (Zechariah 2:8).

Prayer is the most powerful weapon in heaven's arsenal. God answers prayer. Israel is the key to America's survival. September 11th would never have happened if America had stood with Israel over the years, rather than weakening her by rewarding terrorists like Arafat. We must not send a signal to would-be terrorists that crime pays, and that America is weak. 22 years ago, Israel stood up to the nations of the world and blew up the Iraqi Osirak nuclear reactor. The entire world, including America, condemned Israel for it. Israel's courageous act may have saved millions of American lives on September 11th.

In 1980, I did an interview with Isser Harel, head of Mossad, Israeli intelligence, from 1947-1963. *The Jerusalem Post* published an article on that interview on September 30, 2001. The article entitled, "America: the Target" will help you understand the seriousness of the matter:

> *On a September evening in 1980 in Tel Aviv, I sat with former Mossad chief Isser Harel for a conversation about Arab terrorism. As he handed me a cup of hot tea and a plate of cookies, I asked him, "Do you think terrorism will come to America, and if so, where and why?"*
>
> *Harel looked at his American visitor and replied, "I fear it will come to you in America. America has the power, but not the will, to fight*

terrorism. The terrorists have the will, but not the power, to fight America—but all that could change with time. Arab oil money buys more than tents."

As to the where, Harel continued, "New York City is the symbol of freedom and capitalism. It's likely they will strike the Empire State Building, your tallest building [at that time] and a symbol of your power."

With my Western mind-set I replied that America was dedicated to fighting terrorism. Harel smiled and said, "You kill a fly and you celebrate. We live with flies daily. One dies and 100 flies come to the funeral."

"If 'land for peace' happens," Harel continued, "I think it will mean America gets peace for a season, as the West pressures Israel into giving Arafat our land. But once you let the genie of appeasement out of the bottle, he will grow and eventually turn on you. In time America itself will be in the crosshairs."

"Hitler first killed Jews, then he killed Christians. Our culture and our democracies are the root of [the terrorists'] rage. If we're right, then they are wrong."

Twenty-one years later, the first part of Harel's prediction came true; except, of course, that the twin towers of the World Trade Center *were much taller than the Empire State Building. However, it was the second part of his doomsday prediction that came true much earlier.*

It was 1982 and Israel had declared its own war on terrorism by invading Lebanon to root out Arafat's terrorist infrastructure. I was summoned to New York by Prime Minister Menachem Begin's aide, Reuven Hecht, for a meeting with Begin prior to his meeting with President Ronald Reagan. Hecht had just met in Washington with secretary of state Alexander Haig, who had told him that America had changed its mind: it would no longer support Israel's war against terrorism in Lebanon.

Begin was in shock. The West—whose planes had been blown out of the sky, its diplomats, soldiers, and civilians murdered by terrorists—was now fighting to save the primary organization responsible for these vile acts. In the end, American pressure prevailed and Arafat's 10,000 PLO terrorists, rifles in hand, were escorted out of Beirut to safe bases in Tunisia and other Arab lands. The cries of Israeli mothers whose sons had died in Lebanon and who stood outside his apartment screaming "Murderer!" were more than Begin could bear. He resigned a depressed and broken man.

Since then hundreds of Israeli civilians have

been killed and thousands wounded by terrorists recruited, trained and equipped in territory controlled by Arafat's Palestinian Authority. Osama bin Laden's cells operated in the West Bank and Gaza Strip, as did Hezbollah—all with Arafat's blessing.

After declaring his own war against terrorism, Arafat summoned the press to photograph him giving blood ostensibly for the victims of the attacks on America. Meanwhile, his Palestinian Police threatened journalists who filmed Palestinians dancing in the streets to celebrate the 9/11 attacks... all this supposedly in aid of encouraging Islamic states to join the anti-terrorism coalition.

Even Arafat's Hamas successor announced it was willing to suspend suicide attacks inside Israel "unless provoked." Can you imagine someone like the late Osama bin Laden saying, "I will suspend suicide attacks against America unless I am provoked—now let me join the anti-terrorism coalition"?

Israel and America share the same democratic values that terrorists despise and seek to destroy. For Americans to think that Arafat, the godfather of Islamic terrorism, did not continue to support it is absurd. He advocated bringing more terror to America. Arafat's supporters, the

Liberal Left in the U.S. believed (and still believes) that some terrorists can be categorized as good and some as bad. This is a guarantee for failure.

I was so convinced Harel was right, that in 1999, I wrote a novel called *The Jerusalem Scroll* in which Osama bin Laden obtains a nuclear bomb from the Russian mafia and attempts to blow up New York City and Los Angeles. Little did I know he would attempt both misdeeds. But thank God, he did not have a nuclear bomb.

An amazing Scripture in the Bible is found in Luke 7:5 (KJV): *"For he loveth our Nation, and hath built us a synagogue."* The Jewish Elders made an appeal to Jesus to come and heal the servant of Cornelius in Capernaum, for he was close to death. This was a Gentile. The Jews said to Jesus, "he deserves a blessing because he has been a blessing. He has performed some wonderful deeds of compassion for our people."

A similar story is found in Acts 10. The first Gentile was selected by God in Caesarea to receive the Gospel. Why? The answer is given repeatedly in the book of Acts. In chapter 10, verse 2, *"A devout man (Cornelius) and one who feared God with all his household, who gave alms generously to the people, and prayed to God always."* Who were the people to whom Cornelius gave these alms? They were the

Jews! Acts 10:4: *"…Your prayers and your alms have come up for a memorial before God."* Again in Acts 10:31: *"…your prayer has been heard, and your alms are remembered in the sight of God."* Three times in the same chapter, a godly Gentile expressed his unconditional love for the Jewish people in a practical way. Then Cornelius was divinely selected by God to be the first Gentile house to receive the Gospel, and the first to receive the outpouring of the Holy Spirit.

There is no doubt that prosperity (Genesis 12:3 and Psalm 122:6) and healing (Luke 7:1-5) came first to the Gentiles. The Jewish people and the nation of Israel were blessed in a practical way. They received a Commanded Blessing.

I Will Bless You

Why Christians should wholeheartedly support the Jewish people and their beloved country, Israel, is a selfish reason in some respects, but a valid one nonetheless. After promising Abraham that He would make his offspring a great nation, the God of Israel pledged that He would *"bless those who bless you"* (Genesis 12:3). Of course, Abraham's descendants include the Arab peoples through Ishmael and Esau, and there is every reason for Christians to bless the Arabs today. But we have already seen that God's eternal covenant was passed down to Isaac, Jacob, and the 12 tribes of Israel. This means that the blessing promised by the God of Israel would come to those who particularly blessed the Jewish people.

How can we bless the Jews? There are many ways this can be done. One of the most important and obvious ways is to support their God-given right to live in their Biblical Promised Land, and especially in their eternal capital city, Jerusalem. The sad fact is that many governments, international organizations, Muslim groups and even some Christians do not acknowledge that divine right. For Christians, this unbiblical stand weakens our testimony, weakens the nation of Israel, weakens America, and puts the souls of our nation in harm's way. Dare we call it a conspiracy?

Failure or refusal to support the Jews and their right to return to their ancient homeland can cause us to miss the blessings of God. But it can do more than this, it also places us in danger of being cursed by our Creator. God Himself warns humanity of this danger: *"And the one who curses you, I will curse"* (Genesis 12:3).

By contesting the right of Jews to live in their covenant land, and thereby going against God's holy Word, many are opening themselves up to be cursed! Therefore, anyone who seeks the blessings bestowed by our Heavenly Father should make sure they are obeying His command to bless His special covenant people.

God not only promised to reward individuals for blessing His covenant Jewish people, but He also pledged in the same Scripture to bless families, and by extension, entire nations: *"And in you all the families of the earth shall be blessed."* So the great Master of the Universe reveals that our personal, family, and national welfare is closely related to how we treat the called-out Jewish people. Should anyone need any other reason to support the contemporary offspring of Abraham, Isaac, and Jacob, especially in their brave endeavors to establish a thriving modern state within their Biblically-designated ancestral borders?

Be Blessed!

As we have seen, both the Old and New Testaments make abundantly clear that Christians must support Israel in every possible way. This does not mean that the Israeli people and their government are perfect. Far from it: They are fallen human beings like everyone else on Earth, in desperate need of salvation. But the Biblical prophets, including the Apostle Paul, foretold that the restored Jewish remnant in the Lord's land would mourn over their sins in the Last Days and be grafted back into their own sacred tree.

While waiting, working, and praying for "all Israel to be saved, "we must wholeheartedly support what the sovereign Lord is doing in returning His ancient covenant people back to their God-given land. In doing so, we will be blessed as they are blessed. And best of all, we will make our eternal Father happy by obeying His revealed will on a matter that is clearly close to His heart.

"Thus says the Lord: 'Against all My evil neighbors who touch the inheritance which I have caused My people Israel to inherit—behold, I will pluck them out of their land and pluck out the house of Judah from among them" (Jeremiah 12:14).

When we refuse to pray, we are saying simply, "God, I know better than you. I will not obey Your Word." God's Word says, *"I have written my name there…."* Almighty God has promised to dwell with them in the land (Zechariah 2:10). God will determine blessings or curses on nations depending on how they treat Israel.

"Now the LORD had said unto Abram, Get thee out of thy country, and from thy kindred, and from thy father's house, unto a land that I will shew thee: And I will make of thee a great

nation, and I will bless thee, and make thy name great; and thou shalt be a blessing: **And I will bless them that bless thee, and curse him that curseth thee: and in thee shall all families of the earth be blessed**" (Genesis 12:1-3, KJV).

"And the LORD said unto Abram, after that Lot was separated from him, Lift up now thine eyes, and look from the place where thou art northward, and southward, and eastward, and westward: **For all the land which thou seest, to thee will I give it, and to thy seed for ever.** And I will make thy seed as the dust of the earth: so that if a man can number the dust of the earth, then shall thy seed also be numbered. Arise, walk through the land in the length of it and in the breadth of it; for I will give it unto thee. Then Abram removed his tent, and came and dwelt in the plain of Mamre, which is in Hebron, and built there an altar unto the LORD" (Genesis 13:14-18, KJV).

"As for me, behold, my covenant is with thee, and thou shalt be a father of many nations. Neither shall thy name any more be called Abram, but thy name shall be Abraham; for a father of many nations have I made thee. And I will make thee exceeding fruitful, and I will make nations of thee, and kings shall come out of thee. And I will establish my covenant between me and thee and thy seed after thee in their generations for **an everlasting covenant**, to be a God unto thee, and to thy seed after thee. And I will give unto thee, and to thy seed after thee, the land wherein thou art a stranger, all the land of Canaan, for an everlasting possession; and I will be their God" (Genesis 17:4-8, KJV).

"And the angel of the LORD called unto Abraham out of heaven the second time, And said, By myself have I sworn, saith the LORD, for because thou hast done this thing, and hast not withheld thy son, thine only son: That in blessing I will bless thee, and in multiplying I will multiply thy seed as the stars of the heaven, and as the sand which is upon the sea shore; and thy seed shall possess the gate of his enemies; **And in thy seed shall all the nations of the earth be blessed**; because thou hast obeyed my voice" (Genesis 22:15-18, KJV).

"And there was a famine in the land, beside the first famine that was in the days of Abraham. And Isaac went unto Abimelech king of the Philistines unto Gerar. And the LORD appeared unto him, and said, Go not down into Egypt; dwell in the land which I shall tell thee of: Sojourn in this land, and I will be with thee, and will bless thee; for unto thee, and unto thy *seed, I will give all these countries, and I will perform the oath which I sware unto Abraham thy father; And I will make thy seed to multiply as the stars of heaven, and will give unto thy seed all these countries; and in thy seed shall all the nations of the earth be blessed; Because that Abraham obeyed my voice, and kept my charge, my commandments, my statutes, and my laws"* (Genesis 26:1-5, KJV).

2. Because Israel—and Jerusalem in particular—is the Heart and Soul of the Jewish People and God Has Chosen it as His Earthly Capital

"Yet I have chosen Jerusalem, that My name may be there..." (2 Chronicles 6:6).

All the expressions of Divine love still hold true for Israel today; none of them have been canceled. Israel is, and always will be, the apple of God's eye (Zechariah 2:8). She remains God's joy and delight, His royal diadem (Isaiah 62:3), His firstborn, His Chosen One, His beloved (Jeremiah 2:2, Hosea 11:1). Indeed, He says of His people, *"For they shall be like the jewels of a crown"* (Zechariah 9:16).

"He will set up a banner for the nations, And will assemble the outcasts of Israel, And gather together the dispersed of Judah From the four corners of the earth" (Isaiah 11:12).

"The Lord also will roar from Zion, And utter His voice from Jerusalem; The heavens and earth will shake; But the Lord will be a shelter for His people, And the strength of the children of Israel" (Joel 3:16).

"Those who trust in the Lord Are like Mount Zion, Which cannot be moved, but abides forever. As the mountains surround Jerusalem, So the Lord surrounds His people From this time forth and forever" (Psalm 125:1-2).

"Then I, John, saw the holy city, New

Jerusalem, coming down out of heaven from God, prepared as a bride adorned for her husband" (Revelation 21:2).

"For thus says the Lord of hosts: "He sent Me after glory, to the nations which plunder you; for he who touches you touches the apple of His eye" (Zechariah 2:8).

"'For I,' says the Lord, 'will be a wall of fire all around her, and I will be the glory in her midst.'" (Zechariah 2:5).

When you sign your name to a check, it represents that you possess the amount indicated on that check. God wrote His name in Jerusalem, and He has the power to possess what His name represents.

"This is the word of the LORD concerning Israel. The LORD, who stretches out the heavens, who lays the foundation of the earth, and who forms the spirit of man within him, declares: 'I am going to make Jerusalem a cup that sends all the surrounding peoples reeling. Judah will be besieged as well as Jerusalem. On that day, when all the nations of the earth are gathered against her, I will make Jerusalem an immovable rock for all the nations. All who try to move it will injure themselves. On that day I will strike every horse with panic and its rider with madness,' declares the LORD. 'I will keep a watchful eye over the house of Judah, but I will

blind all the horses of the nations. Then the lead-
ers of Judah will say in their hearts, "The people
of Jerusalem are strong, because the LORD
Almighty is their God." 'On that day I will
make the leaders of Judah like a firepot in a
woodpile, like a flaming torch among sheaves.
They will consume right and left all the sur-
rounding peoples, but Jerusalem will remain
intact in her place" (Zechariah 12:1-6, NIV).

"In the last days the mountain of the
LORD's temple will be established as chief
among the mountains; it will be raised above the
hills, and all nations will stream to it. Many
peoples will come and say, 'Come, let us go up
to the mountain of the LORD, to the house of
the God of Jacob. He will teach us his ways, so
that we may walk in his paths.' The law will go
out from Zion, the word of the LORD from
Jerusalem. He will judge between the nations
and will settle disputes for many peoples. They
will beat their swords into plowshares and their
spears into pruning hooks. Nation will not take
up sword against nation, nor will they train for
war anymore" (Isaiah 2:2-4, NIV).

On July 30, 1980, the Israeli Knesset voted to
affirm a united Jerusalem as the capital of the State
of Israel. Shortly afterward, I had the privilege of
sitting down with the man who had become my

dear friend, Prime Minister Menachem Begin. We talked about the vastness of the territory held by Israel's enemies. It seemed inconceivable to me that Arab countries are 650 times the size of Israel, and that by comparison, Israel is the size of New Jersey; the Arab countries are the size of the entire United States, all of Mexico, and Central America combined. For instance:

- Arab dictators control 13,486,861 square kilometers in the Middle East, and Israel controls 20,770 (Palestinefacts.org).
- The population of Israel is roughly 7.8 million, compared to the population of 300 million living in the surrounding Arab countries.
- The Arab nations are represented by 21 separate countries.[i]

To this day, the vast majority of nations do not recognize Jerusalem as the capital of Israel. In our discussions, I said to Mr. Begin, "How can this be possible when so many people in America and the world believe the Bible?" Mr. Begin just smiled that enigmatic smile of his. As we talked, I told him about a publication that had come into my possession from the Egyptian state information service, "Jerusalem, an Arab City." It had been printed by *al-Ahram* press in Cairo. The book stated on page eight, "Jerusalem was invaded by Christian Arabs in the year 90 B.C. and remained under their domination until it was occupied by the Romans in the first century A.D."[ii]

Of course, both of us were well aware that the Arab world's claim to Jerusalem was based on misinformation. How could a state publication declare a right to Jerusalem based on the presumption that Christian Arabs had invaded Jerusalem 90 years *before* the birth of Christ? It is this type of propaganda that floods the Arab world feeding and fueling the hatred for the Jewish people.

The prime minister answered my unasked question. "Being a student of the Bible, you know that almost 3,000 years ago King David united the Kingdoms of Judea and Israel. He transferred the seat of power from Hebron to Jerusalem, where he ruled for 33 years. He wanted to build the Temple on Mount Moriah, where Abraham was to offer his son, Isaac, as a sacrifice.

"David petitioned God to be allowed to build a home for Him in Jerusalem. God answered, *'You have shed much blood and have made great wars; you shall not build a house for My name, because you have shed much blood on the earth in My sight'* (I Chronicles 22:8). God promised David a son who would follow after him as king and would build the Temple. Since then, Jerusalem has been the capital of the Jewish state… one of the oldest capital cities in the world."

The Prime Minister was aware there were detractors who refused to recognize Israel, much less Jerusalem as its capital city. "We came to Camp David to make peace with Egypt and one of your statesmen told me that the government of the United States did not recognize Jerusalem as the capital of Israel. I answered, 'Whether you recognize or don't recognize, Jerusalem is the capital of the State of Israel.'

"After the Six Day War, we liberated the eastern part of Jerusalem from Jordanian occupation. For 19 years we couldn't go to the Western Wall to pray. That was the only time since the [second] Temple had been destroyed by the Romans. Under all other regimes we were free to go to the Western Wall to pray, but the Jordanians didn't allow us passage, in breach of the arms agreement.

"The Olive Mountain Cemetery in which our greatest sages are buried for centuries was completely desecrated. Monuments were destroyed and turned into floors of places which are unmentionable. I will not even use the names [latrines]. All of our synagogues were destroyed...the Jewish Quarter, which was centuries old was leveled.

"Under our jurisdiction, we reconsecrated the Olive Mountain Cemetery and everyone has access to the Holy Shrines—the Holy Sepulchre, the Church of the Nativity. A Muslim goes to the mosque to pray in absolute safety.

"Here in Jerusalem is the government, the Parliament, the president, the Supreme Court. Whoever says, either on behalf of a great power or of a small country, 'We can't recognize Jerusalem as the capital of Israel,' my reply is always the same: 'Excuse me, sir, but we don't recognize your non-recognition.'"

The prime minister's comments brought to mind something Moshe Dayan said during his address to the 34th General Assembly of the United Nations in September 1979. "Jerusalem has known many foreign rulers during the course of its long history, but none of them regarded it as their capital. Only the Jewish people have always maintained it as the sole center of its national and spiritual life. For thousands of years Jews have prayed daily for their return to Jerusalem, and for the past century and a half, Jerusalem has had a continuous and uninterrupted Jewish majority." [iii]

Jerusalem is the symbol of all that Israel represents in our world. Teddy Kollek, Jerusalem's first mayor wrote, "Jerusalem, this beautiful, golden city, is the heart and soul of the Jewish people. One cannot live without a heart and soul. If you want one single word to symbolize all of Jewish history, that word is Jerusalem." [iv]

Out of the long negotiations to establish a Jewish homeland a friendship grew between Dr. Chaim

Weizmann, a Jewish statesman, and Lord Balfour, British foreign secretary. Balfour was unable to understand why the Jews were insisting they would only accept Palestine as their permanent homeland. One day Lord Balfour asked Dr. Weizmann for an explanation. "Mr. Balfour, let's suppose I propose that you replace London with Paris, would you accept?"

A surprised Balfour responded, "But, London is ours!"

Replied Weizmann, "Jerusalem was ours when London was still a swampland."[v]

The very name evokes a stirring in the heart and soul. It has been called by many names: City of God, City of David, Zion, the City of the Great King, Ariel (Lion of God), Moriah (chosen of the Lord). But only one name resonates down through the centuries—Jerusalem! David's city!

A world map drawn in 1581 has Jerusalem at its very center with the then-known continents of the world surrounding it. It resembles a ship's propeller with the shaft in the center being Jerusalem. Another analogy is of Jerusalem as the navel of the earth.

Jerusalem history can be summed up in one word—troubled! Lying as it did between the rival empires of Egypt to the south and Syria to the north, both striving for dominance in the region, Israel was constantly trampled by the opposing armies. It has been conquered at various times by the Canaanites, Jebusites, Babylonians, Assyrians, Persians, Romans, Byzantines, Arabs, Crusaders, Ottomans, and the British. While its origins are lost in the hazy mists of antiquity, archaeological evidence of human habitation goes back some 4,000 years. Jerusalem is first mentioned in Joshua 10:1.

We read there that Adoni-Zedek was the king of Jerusalem and fought unsuccessfully against Joshua. The Israelites first occupied Jerusalem during the days of the Judges (1:21), but did not completely inhabit the city until 1049 B.C. when David wrested it from the Jebusites and declared it the capital city of the Jewish people.

In *Jerusalem, Sacred City of Mankind*, Teddy Kollek and Moshe Pearlman wrote, "The spiritual attachment of the Jews to Jerusalem has remained unbroken; it is a unique attachment. Should one doubt that statement, he would have to look long and hard to find another relationship in history where a people, even in captivity, remained so passionately attached to a city for 3,000 years."[vi]

When the Jews were driven from their land at various times, wherever they found themselves in exile, they faced toward Jerusalem when praying. After Nebuchadnezzar signed a decree making it illegal to pray to anyone except him, Daniel 6:10

says, *"Now when Daniel knew that the writing was signed, he went home. And in his upper room, with his windows open toward Jerusalem, he knelt down on his knees three times that day, and prayed and gave thanks before his God, as was his custom since early days."*

Jewish synagogues faced Jerusalem. When a Jew built a house part of a wall was left unfinished to symbolize that it was only a temporary dwelling—until he could return to his permanent home, Jerusalem. Even the traditional smashing of a glass during a wedding ceremony has its roots in the Temple in Jerusalem. This act of remembering the loss of the center of Jewish festivities during the marriage feast sets *"Jerusalem above [their] highest joy"* (Psalm 137:6, KJV).

When compared with the great cities of the world, Jerusalem is small. It stands alongside no great river as do London, Paris, or Rome. It boasts no port, no major industries, no mineral wealth or even an adequate water supply. The city doesn't stand on a major thoroughfare connected to the rest of the world. Why then is Jerusalem the naval of the earth, the shaft that propels the world ever forward?

The answer can be found in its spiritual significance. Jerusalem is the home of two of the world's monotheistic faiths—Judaism and Christianity, and is claimed by a third—Islam. Biblical prophets proclaimed that from Jerusalem the Word of the Lord would go out to the world—a Word, which would change the moral standards of all mankind.

The spiritual stature of Jerusalem is echoed in its physical situation; it stands upon the Judean hills high above the surrounding countryside. Traveling to Jerusalem is always spoken of as "going up to Jerusalem." Those who leave the City of God are said to "go down"—in perhaps more than just the physical sense.

When viewing the history of Jerusalem as a whole, no other city has suffered as has David's City. At times the city was overrun by violent assailants. It is recorded in Jeremiah that the city would surrender after suffering the horrors of starvation—and be reduced to cannibalism (Jeremiah 19).

While Christian and Muslim claims to Jerusalem came much later, the story of the Jews in Jerusalem began three millennia ago, and has never ceased. The link of the Jewish people has been historical, religious, cultural, physical, and fundamental. It has never been voluntarily broken; any absence of the Jews from their beloved city has been the result of foreign persecution and expulsion. To the Jews alone belongs David's City, the City of God.

For the Jewish people whose cry for centuries has been, "Next year Jerusalem," it is more than a location on the map, it is not just a tourist Mecca where one can visit various holy sites; Jerusalem *is* holy. It is the essence of all for which the Jews have hoped and prayed and cried and died. It is their God-given land.

> "...the LORD had said to David and to Solomon his son, 'In this house and in Jerusalem, which I have chosen out of all the tribes of Israel, I will put My name forever'" (2 Kings 21:7).

Israel is *God's* Dream; the title deed belongs to Him. It is His to bestow on whomever He will—and He has given the right of occupation to the Jewish people. When God made His eternal promises to Israel, there was no United Nations, no United States, no Russia, no European Union, and no Arab League; there were only pagan nations to challenge this dream, to challenge God and His Word. Today, those same pagan voices are challenging the right of the Jews to occupy a unified Jerusalem.

When you and I as Christians are apathetic toward God's divine plan or His eternal purpose, it means that we are rejecting our Lord's divine assignment to the Church. God's prophetic time clock has been set on Jerusalem time throughout history, and the spotlight of heaven is still on the Jews as His Chosen People. It began with them, and it will end with them.

We embrace the name of Christ and serve the

God of Abraham, Isaac, and Jacob. We heed the warnings of the prophets Isaiah, Jeremiah, Ezekiel, Daniel, Hosea, and Joel. We sing the Psalms of King David and find hope. The mention of Jerusalem quickens our hearts for it is our spiritual city. We support our Jewish brothers and sisters in their fight against anti-Semitism and the threat of terrorism.

God's plan is an eternal one! As Christians, we cannot afford to neglect our responsibility to stand with the House of Israel. It is as important as it is to believe the promises of God. As Christians, we are the engrafted vine; we bow before a Jewish Messiah; and what we do matters in the light of eternity.

Jerusalem is the only city for which God commands us to pray. He also commands a blessing on those who pray for Jerusalem! When you pray for Jerusalem as instructed in Psalm 122:6, you are not praying for stones or dirt, you are praying for revival (2 Chronicles 7:14), and for the Lord's return. Also, you are joining our Lord, the Good Samaritan, in His ministry of love and comfort to the suffering. *"Inasmuch as you did it to one of the least of these My brethren, you did it to Me"* (Matthew 25:40).

This is our divine commission.

King David explained precisely why God Almighty has commanded us to pray for the peace of Jerusalem, and has commanded a blessing upon us for doing so. The revelation is found in Psalm

122:8: *"For the sake of my brethren and companions, I will now say, 'Peace be within you.'"* God is telling us to pray for the peace of the inhabitants of Jerusalem. David felt that prayer needed to be offered up for all of his brothers, and friends who lived there. Prayer needs to be offered today for the House of Israel and for peace for those who reside there from the over 120 nations of the world. It is the city most targeted by terrorists, simply because of hatred for the Jewish people and the significance of Jerusalem to them. It has drawn the Jewish people of the world like a prophetic magnet—those who have prayed, "Next year in Jerusalem."

In Psalm 122:9, David's revelation says, *"Because of the house of the LORD our God I will seek your good."* When we pray for the peace of Jerusalem, we are ultimately praying for Satan to be bound. In Isaiah 14, Satan said he would battle God from the Temple of the Lord, on the sides of the north. When we pray for the peace of Jerusalem, we are praying for those who live there, and we are praying for the Messiah to come. The prophecies of the Bible point to the Temple of the Lord as the key flashpoint that will bring the nations of the world to Jerusalem, and result in the battle that will end Satan's reign over the earth for all eternity. It will spell his final defeat!

In 691 A.D., Islamic adherents of the Umayyad dynasty began a campaign to "exalt and glorify"[vii] the city of Jerusalem. Umayyad Caliph Abd al-Malik built the Dome of the Rock over the Foundation Stone, the Holy of Holies. It was thought to have been erected in direct competition with Christianity. The edifice still stands today. Islam later attributed another event to the Foundation Stone: the binding of the son of Abraham the "Hanif," the first Monotheist. As the Koran does not explicitly mention the name Isaac, commentators on the Koran have identified the son bound by Abraham as Ishmael. Thus Islam teaches that the title deed to Jerusalem and the Temple Site and all of Israel belong to the Arabs—not the Jews.

In fact, Mohammed never set foot in Jerusalem, nor is the city mentioned by name in the Koran. His only connection to Jerusalem is through his dream or vision where he found himself in a "temple that is most remote" (Koran, Sura). It was not until the 7th Century that Muslim adherents identified the "temple most remote" as a mosque in Jerusalem (perhaps for political reasons).

The truth remains that this site on which now stands the Dome of the Rock, and is sacred to Jews as the Temple site, will be the basis for the battle of ages that will be fought.

There is a divine reason the Church was born in Zion! All roads lead to Jerusalem, Judea, and Samaria. The world is hopeless, not knowing what to do. Heaven and Earth met in Jerusalem, and will meet there again. The destiny of America and the world is linked to Jerusalem. It is the epicenter of spiritual warfare and affects the entire world.

Jerusalem, Judea, and Samaria are the battle zones. It is no accident that the Great Commission is directed toward these prophetic areas. If Christians are not salt and light, then the Great Commission will become the Great Omission! *"But ye shall receive power, after that the Holy Ghost is come upon you: and ye shall be witnesses unto me both in Jerusalem, and in all Judaea, and in Samaria, and unto the uttermost part of the earth"* (Acts 1:8, KJV).

If our Lord and Savior reached out in compassion to Israel, and made prayer for her His highest priority, do we dare make it our lowest? There is a direct correlation between the power that Heaven promised for the Church at its birth in Jerusalem, and the Church's obedience to be a witness in Jerusalem, Judea, and Samaria. The Church cannot, and must not, ignore Christ's eternal mission for her, and at the same time, expect power from on high. If His disciples' obedience was directly related to a power surge from Heaven and the birth of the Church, can disobedience empower the Church and lift her heavenward to fulfill her final mission?

"Arise, shine; for thy light is come, and the glory of the LORD is risen upon thee. For,

behold, the darkness shall cover the earth, and gross darkness the people: but the LORD shall arise upon thee, and his glory shall be seen upon thee. And the Gentiles shall come to thy light, and kings to the brightness of thy rising." (Isaiah 60:1-3, KJV)

Jerusalem: God's Capital City

Another significant reason why Christians should rejoice in Israel's physical restoration and strongly support her continued existence in the Middle East is the prophesied future of her ancient and modern capital city, Jerusalem. Holy writ reveals that Zion is to be the very seat of the Messiah's earthly reign. The nations on earth will come up to visit Jerusalem when Jesus rules from the holy city as King of Kings and Lord of Lords! This is revealed in several Scriptures:

"Many people shall come and say, 'Come, and let us go up to the mountain of the Lord, To the house of the God of Jacob; He will teach us His ways, And we shall walk in His paths.' For out of Zion shall go forth the law, And the word of the Lord from Jerusalem" (Isaiah 2:3).

"Look upon Zion, the city of our appointed feasts; Your eyes will see Jerusalem, a quiet home, A tabernacle that will not be taken down;

Not one of its stakes will ever be removed, Nor will any of its cords be broken." (Isaiah 33:20).

"Thus says the Lord, 'I will return to Zion, And will dwell in the midst of Jerusalem. Jerusalem shall be called the City of Truth, The Mountain of the Lord of hosts, The Holy Mountain.'" (Zechariah 8:3).

"I will not give sleep to mine eyes, Or slumber to mine eyelids, Until I find out a place for the LORD, an habitation for the Mighty One of Jacob…For Your servant David's sake, Do not turn away the face of Your Anointed…For the LORD has chosen Zion; He has desired it for His dwelling place. 'This is my resting place forever; Here I will dwell, for I have desired it'" (Psalm 132:4-5, 10, 13-14).

*"Moreover I will appoint a place for My people Israel, and will plant them, that they may dwell in a place of their own, and **MOVE NO MORE**; nor shall the children of wickedness oppress them any more, as previously"* (2 Samuel 7:10).

It is evident from Scripture that the Sovereign Lord of Creation has chosen the city of Jerusalem as His earthly capital. This decision was made by the very same God who promised to restore His covenanted Jewish people to the sacred city and surrounding land in the last days before the Second

Coming. How can Christians look for and welcome Jesus' prophesied return, and not rejoice in and actively support the Jewish return that was foretold to at least partially precede it?

God described the details and boundaries of the land in Genesis 15:18: *"On the same day the Lord made a covenant with Abram, saying: 'To your descendants I have given this land, from the river of Egypt to the great river, the River Euphrates."* This was a royal land grant, perpetual and unconditional. Genesis 17:8: *"Also I give to you and your descendants after you the land in which you are a stranger, all the land of Canaan, as an everlasting possession; and I will be their God."* Genesis 28:13: *"the land on which you lie I will give to you and your descendants."* God has never revoked Abraham's title deed to the land, nor has He given it to anyone else.

The spot where God confirmed His covenant is an area north of Jerusalem between Bethel and Ai. It is in the heart of what is called the West Bank, or Judea and Samaria. (The United Nations refers to this as "occupied territory," and demands that Israel relinquish it.) An inalienable right is one that cannot be given away. The Bible declares this to be so in Leviticus 25:23. The people were forbidden to sell the land because, *'The land must not be sold permanently, because the land is mine and you are but aliens and my tenants."*

Jerusalem is the only city God claims as His own; it is called the City of God and the Holy City in Scripture. He declared to Solomon in 2 Chronicles 33:7, *"In this house and in Jerusalem, which I have chosen out of all the tribes of Israel, I will put my Name forever."*

In October of 1991 the Middle East peace conference was convened at the Royal Palace in Madrid, Spain. I was sent by God to be a witness there. I was the first person to speak after Secretary of State James Baker concluded his remarks. I asked, "Why can't America recognize Jerusalem as Israel's capital? Secondly, we are moving a military presence into the Arab world for security. Why can't we have a military presence in Israel to help its security? It has suffered so greatly, and has especially paid a dear price during the Persian Gulf War." Baker was incensed by my remarks and said he refused to be entangled in a fruitless debate and that the status of Jerusalem should be determined by negotiations.

To this day, America has refused to recognize Jerusalem as Israel's capital. This is a grave mistake. I have shouted this warning from the White House in Washington to the Royal Palace in Madrid as I rebuked world leaders with the words, "God does not recognize America's non-recognition position!"

3. Because When We Support Israel, We are Preparing for Our Lord's Coming!

"For the Lord shall build up Zion; He shall appear in his glory!" (Psalm 102:16)

When we pray for Jerusalem we are saying, "Maranatha, come Messiah!" The Messiah is indeed coming back, and He is coming to Jerusalem. That is something on which both Jews and Christians agree. As Christians, we believe that we know His name, while the Jewish people say they don't. But there is no question that when Messiah comes, everyone will know His name.

Our Lord was asked by His disciples in Matthew 24:3, "*And what will be the sign of Your coming, and of the end of the age?*" He clearly gave them the signs beginning with the destruction of the Temple. In verse 2, Jesus prophesied that the Temple would be taken apart stone by stone 40 years before it happened. The fig tree has always been a symbol of the Nation of Israel. In verses 32-36, Jesus laid out the key sign of His return, and the end of the age...the sign of the fig tree. That "fig tree" bloomed on May 14, 1948, in fulfillment of Isaiah 66:8: "*Shall the earth be made to give birth in one day? Or shall a nation be born at once?*" Jesus warned to not set dates for "*no one would know the day or the hour.*" He also said that the generation which saw the blooming of the fig tree would not pass away until He came.

It was 597 B.C., in the days of Nebuchadnezzar in Babylon (now modern-day Iraq) that Israel was taken into captivity. Since then, Israel has changed hands 26 times. It has been leveled to the ground five times. But in 1948, the prophecy of Matthew 24 knocked at the door.

A generation is most often defined as 70-80 years. If a person had been 10 years old in 1948 when this prophecy was fulfilled, that person would be 73 years old today. There is no question that we will not know that day or the hour, but Matthew 24 seems to indicate that we are very, very close to Messiah's return. The events in the Middle East are surely lining up with this prophecy!

Jesus is coming soon! We had better be sure that what we are living for is worthy of Christ having died for, and that we ask ourselves this simple question: **How will what we do to Israel through our apathy or our actions matter in the light of eternity?**

"For Zion's sake will I not hold my peace, and for Jerusalem's sake I will not rest, until the righteousness thereof go forth as brightness, and the salvation thereof as a lamp that burneth. And the Gentiles shall see thy righteousness, and all kings thy glory: and thou shalt be called by a new name, which the mouth of the LORD

*shall name. Thou shalt also be a crown of glory
in the hand of the LORD, and a royal diadem in
the hand of thy God. Thou shalt no more be
termed Forsaken; neither shall thy land any
more be termed Desolate: but thou shalt be called
Hephzibah, and thy land Beulah: for the LORD
delighteth in thee, and thy land shall be married.
For as a young man marrieth a virgin, so shall
thy sons marry thee: and as the bridegroom
rejoiceth over the bride, so shall thy God rejoice
over thee. I have set watchmen upon thy walls,
O Jerusalem, which shall never hold their peace
day nor night: ye that make mention of the
LORD, keep not silence, And give him no rest,
till he establish, and till he make Jerusalem a
praise in the earth"* (Isaiah 62:1-7, KJV).

Christians have a date with destiny! The
Church cannot fulfill its eternal purpose if it is not
salt and light unto Israel (Acts 1:8). When we support Israel, we are supporting the only nation that
was created by an act of God: The royal land grant
that was given to Abraham and his seed through
Isaac and Jacob, with an everlasting and unconditional covenant.

*"My mercy will I keep for him for evermore,
and my covenant shall stand fast with him. His
seed also will I make to endure for ever, and his
throne as the days of heaven. If his children for-*

sake my law, and walk not in my judgments; If they break my statutes, and keep not my commandments; then will I visit their transgression with the rod, and their iniquity with stripes. Nevertheless my loving kindness will I not utterly take from him, nor suffer my faithfulness to fail. My covenant will I not break, nor alter the thing that is gone out of my lips. Once have I sworn by my holiness that I will not lie unto David. His seed shall endure forever, and his throne as the sun before me. It shall be established forever as the moon, and as a faithful witness in heaven. Selah" (Psalm 89:28-37).

On December 12, 1988, the United Nations invited Yasser Arafat to speak in Geneva. The goal was to unify the world behind his plan for a PLO state in Israel. He was asked to simply say the words, "I denounce terrorism." He did…not only there, but thousands of times before his death, mostly after terrorist bombers had blown up Jews under his orders and with his financing.

At the UN meeting, I confronted Arafat and said, "Jerusalem is Israel's capital, according to the Bible. We believe the Messiah is coming back to Jerusalem, which will be in the hands of the Jews when He comes." Arafat started screaming, "Shut up! Shut up! What must I do to make you shut up? Shall I strip tease for you? It would be absurd."

The Nation of Israel heard his words. The following day, I was asked to speak up for Israel after their meeting. I lifted my Bible heavenward and declared, "This is the final Word. It's non-negotiable. The land belongs to God Almighty, and He alone has decided its destiny."

At Camp David in July 2000, President Bill Clinton almost succeeded in dividing Jerusalem. He placed the pen in the hands of Arafat to sign the agreement that would have accomplished that. Arafat would not sign; the President was in shock. If Arafat had, Jerusalem would have been divided. All Christian sites would then be under Islamic rule of law! This includes Mount Calvary and the Garden Tomb, and even the Christians who live there. The Bible says that Jerusalem will be in the hands of the Jewish people when Messiah returns! America was challenging God Almighty and His prophetic plan. Not a wise thing to do!

Why did Arafat not sign the agreement? He wanted ALL of the Temple Site! Why did he not succeed in his efforts to exert control over this site? The sons of Esau live in the desert, and run their oppressive governments by the bullet, not the ballot. Those who take a stand against Israel will be fighting God himself! Arafat could not win in a battle against God Almighty. Why? For thousands of years, their fathers have spoken curses over Jacob's seed. When the wars of the Middle East have ended, Jacob's sons will rule. Who will win the conflict in the Middle East? Those who bless Israel will be triumphant. Who will lose the battle in the Middle East? Those who fight the State of Israel will go down in defeat. God created Israel. God defends Israel.

Consider the nation of Egypt. Joseph birthed a generation of wealth. After his death, there arose a Pharaoh that persecuted the Jewish people, and enslaved them. He not only starved them, but also drowned their children in the Nile River. Why? He was trying to control that nation. As a result of Pharaoh's enslavement of His people, God sent plagues. The first-born child in every Egyptian home was slain by the Death Angel. In some Egyptian homes, that meant every family member died.

For every Hebrew baby that died in the Nile River, an Egyptian child died. For every Hebrew father who died at the oppressive hands of the Egyptian overseers, an Egyptian father died. For every Hebrew mother who died of starvation, or of a broken heart, an Egyptian mother died. What you do to another, God will cause to come to you.

An angry, bitter Pharaoh gathered his terrified, demoralized troops, and pursued the Hebrew children as they departed Egypt. He led his army directly into the path of God's wrath, and all drowned in the Red Sea. Overnight, Egypt became a land of poverty, and disease. It remains that way 4,000 years later…because it chose to curse the Jewish people, rather than bless them.

4. Because God's Word is True.

"For out of Zion shall go forth the law, And the word of the Lord from Jerusalem" (Isaiah 2:3).

The survival of the Jews is a fulfillment of biblical prophecy. If the Jews had not survived, God's Word would not be true! Satan attempted to force Christ to pervert the word of God, but Jesus rebuked him. We must do the same. *"For I am not ashamed of the gospel of Christ, for it is the power of God to salvation…"* (Romans 1:16). Throughout the Bible God has made eternal promises to the people of Israel that He will yet fulfill.

You either believe the entire Bible, or you do not believe any of it. Israel is the fulfillment of Biblical prophecy; she is the apple of God's eye. To purposefully close our eyes to the cries of His people is like willfully and disdainfully poking our finger in God's eye. The fact that the Jewish people exist is a miracle. The rebirth of the Nation of Israel is a miracle. The restoration of the Hebrew language is a miracle, as are the return of the Jewish people to their homeland, and the reunification of Jerusalem.

You either support Israel or you oppose Israel. It's just that simple. Why do we as Christians support Israel? Because God supports Israel, and His Word supports Israel. I have heard some Christians say with pride, "I will not support the Jews in Israel. They are sinners, and the nation is a sinful one." How easily we forget all the mercy God has shown to a sinful America to whom He made not one direct promise. How can we sing, "God Bless America," when this nation leads the world in having killed 54 million babies by abortion since 1967…then curse Israel with our silence and self-righteous attitude?

I seem to remember a Scripture about a Jew who had compassion on Gentiles and said, *"While they were yet sinners, I loved them."* If Christ, a Jew, could love us, can we look in the face of His seed, those He lived with and wept over—and say, "I will not love you"?

"Who has heard such a thing? Who has seen such things? Shall the earth be made to give birth in one day? Or shall a nation be born at once? For as soon as Zion was in labor, She gave birth to her children" (Isaiah 66:8).

"He remembers His covenant forever, The word which He commanded, for a thousand generations, The covenant which He made with Abraham, And His oath to Isaac, And confirmed it to Jacob for a statute, To Israel as an everlasting covenant, Saying, 'To you I will give the land of Canaan As the allotment of your inheritance'" (Psalm 105:8-11).

"I say then, has God cast away His people?

*Certainly not! For I also am an Israelite, of the
seed of Abraham, of the tribe of Benjamin. God
has not cast away His people whom He
foreknew...*" (Romans 11:1-2).

To summarize the 66 books of the Bible in one
word, you only have to say the word "Israel." The
Bible begins with and ends with Israel. There is no
word used more. There are no promises given to
any people more than to Israel. Israel's existence
demonstrates the faithfulness of God, the inspira-
tion and infallibility of the Bible, and the sovereignty of God.

There is a doctrine in vogue spawned by hell,
which teaches that the Church has replaced Israel in
the plan and heart of God. This doctrine is known
alternately as replacement theology, progressive dispensationalism, or supersessionism. The early
Church did not teach this. Its roots date back to the
European Church. The doctrine stated that the
Church has supplanted Israel in God's plan for the
ages, and that the Jews have been rejected. That they
are blind in that they crucified Christ. And that
Israel failed God and as a result was replaced by the
Church. It teaches that the Church is a spiritual
Israel and that Jerusalem is any town in which there
is a church.

To believe that God broke His covenant with
Israel is heresy. You would have to accuse God

Almighty of being a promise breaker! Do you believe God broke His covenant with Abraham, Isaac, or Jacob, and that He would break His covenant with you?

5. Because **Salvation** is of the Jews.

"You worship what you do not know; we know what we worship, for salvation is of the Jews" (John 4:22).

A nother compelling reason for Christians everywhere to enthusiastically support the Jewish people and their modern reborn state is this: Our eternal salvation has come through the agency of the Jews. The fingers of the physical descendants of Jacob wrote all but a small portion of the world's bestselling book: The Bible. The Bible says, *"For if the Gentiles have been partakers of their spiritual things, their duty is also to minister to them in material things"* (Romans 15:27). Christians owe a debt of eternal gratitude to the Jewish people for their contributions that gave birth to our faith. These are only a few of the things that the Jewish people have given to Christianity:

1-The Word of God
2-The Messiah
3-The Patriarchs
4-The Apostles
5-The Disciples

Almost all of the prophets in the Bible were Jewish, as were all of the apostles, the parents of Jesus, and most important, the Messiah Himself.

When speaking to the Samaritan woman about eternal life, Jesus pointed out that His heavenly Father's free gift of eternal salvation has been brought to the world via the Jews: *"You worship that which you do not know; we know what we worship, for **salvation is of the Jews**"* (John 4:22).

If the most precious gift that Christians will ever possess came by means of the Jewish prophets, leaders, teachers, and in particular, the Messiah Jesus, how can we have any attitude other than one of deep gratitude toward Jacob's offspring? We who are Gentiles should be extremely thankful that God, in His shining wisdom and gracious mercy, has allowed us *"wild olive branches"* to be grafted into the rich Tree of Israel, as revealed in Romans 11:17.

In his New Testament letter to the Romans, the Jewish Apostle Paul went on to point out that the *"grafted in"* Gentile Church does not somehow tower over the Jewish people, as many have maintained over the centuries and still do today. Rather, it is the original covenant people that remain the bedrock "root" that supports every Christian's spiritual life: *"...do not boast against the branches. But if you do boast, remember that you do not support the root, but the root supports you"* (Romans 11:18). *"For I am not ashamed of the gospel of Christ: for it is the power of God to salvation to every one who believes, for the Jew first, and also for the Greek"* (Romans 1:16).

I have heard it said, "The reason I don't support Israel is because the Jews crucified Christ. They are under judgment because they rejected God's Word." John 10:17 tells us that Christ willingly gave His life. No one took it from Him: *"Therefore My Father loves Me, because I lay down My life that I may take it again. No one takes it from Me, but I lay it down of Myself. I have power to lay it down, and I have power to take it again"* (John 10:17-18).

God Almighty will judge the person or group that embraces a doctrine of judgment, and who are given the Word, then reject it through disobedience. Nations who reject God will be judged. Luke 12:48 says, *"For everyone to whom much is given, from him much will be required."* There are more churches in America than in any nation in the world. There are more Christian bookstores, more Christian radio and television stations, and more Bible schools.

The world views America as a "Christian nation." Yet, America is the number one Western nation per capita for murder, rape, drugs, alcohol, pornography sales, homosexuality, etc. If this doctrine of judgment is to be meted out, then America is finished as a nation.

The truth is, God is much more merciful than mankind. Lamentations 3:22 states: *"Through the Lord's mercies we are not consumed, Because His com-*

passions fail not." Nowhere in His Word does God make eternal promises to America; yet He continues to show mercy. Even wicked Sodom was to be the beneficiary of God's mercy. Why? Because Abraham appealed to God to spare the city if only ten righteous men could be found there. Regretfully, ten righteous men did not answer the call to stand in the gap.

The Jerusalem Prayer Team is committed to pray for a 2 Chronicles 7:14 revival for America and Israel. This kind of revival can only come through intercessory prayer.

6. Because God Hates Anti-Semitism!

"For he that touches you touches the apple [pupil] of his Eye" (Zechariah 2:8).

Anti-Semitism is hatred against all Jews. Jesus was Jewish, as were the prophets, priests, and kings of Israel in the Bible. Anti-Semitism at its very root is hatred against God, His Son, and His Word. You cannot love Jesus whom you have not seen (who was Jewish) if you don't love the Jewish people whom you have seen. If you refuse to bless the House of Israel when it is in your power to do so, what evidence of true Christian love do you have to present to a Holy God?

Martin Luther King said, *"You declare, my friends, that you do not hate the Jews, you are merely anti-Zionist. And I say, let the truth ring forth from the highest mountaintops. Let it echo through the valleys of God's green earth. When people criticize Zionism, they mean Jews. Zionism is nothing less than the dream and ideal of the Jewish people returning to live in their own land."*

You cannot go to church and talk about how much you love dead Jews, like the ones in the Bible, or the unborn Jews, such as the 144,000 in the Book of Revelation, and not accept the Jews across the street. Neither can you use statements like, "They will Jew you down." That's anti-Semitism, and

God's judgment will come on anyone who touches the seed of Abraham. In the Hebrew, it says, *"Those who speak lightly against you I will visit with heavy blows."*

Christians are Zionists if they believe the Bible. Martin Niemoller, the anti-Nazi theologian and Lutheran pastor wrote in his poem, *First they came,* "In Germany, they first came for the communists, and I didn't speak up because I wasn't a communist. Then they came for the Jews, and I didn't speak up because I wasn't a Jew. Then they came for the trade unionists, and I didn't speak up because I wasn't a trade unionist. Then they came for the Catholics, and I didn't speak up because I wasn't a Catholic. Then they came for me...and by that time there was nobody left to speak up."

In every Arab state, you can buy the book that Hitler used as the excuse to murder six million Jews: *The Protocols of the Learned Elders of Zion.* Why? Because many Muslims are anti-Semitic and believe as Hitler did about the Jews: That all the world's problems are because of the Jews, and that the Jews control the world.

Mother Theresa and I prayed together in Rome for Israel. I remember hearing her words. They are as true today as the day she spoke them: *"You cannot love Jesus without loving the Jewish people."*

Moral and Historical Reasons to Stand with Israel

The awful historical record shows that Jews have been the targets of fierce discrimination and even persecution in "Christian lands" over the centuries. The Vatican-inspired Crusaders deliberately murdered Jewish people during the Middle Ages. The Roman Catholic Inquisitions were directed against the Jews in Spain and elsewhere, leaving many dead or in prison. The pogroms of Russia and Eastern Europe forced Jews from their homes, and left untold numbers dead.

As evil as these anti-Semitic assaults were, they all pale in comparison to the Holocaust of World War II. Some six million Jews perished in "Christian" Europe, at least one million of them children. They were the victims of a cruel regime that had sprung up in the very land where Martin Luther sparked the Protestant Reformation. A full one-third of the entire Jewish race was wiped off the face of God's green earth by Hitler's Nazi forces. The utter horror of the hideous Holocaust as revealed by the testimonies of death-camp survivors cannot be overstressed.

Too late, many Germans recognized the blessings that the Jewish people brought to their society before Hitler's tragic rise to power. Jewish composers, scientists, doctors, teachers, writers, and others contributed their significant talents and intelligence to the land of Luther, and were repaid with Hitler's death chambers. American Christians should be the first to welcome the many contributions and blessings brought to this great land by our Jewish citizens.

During one of my first trips to Israel nearly three decades ago, I spent an afternoon with a brilliant Jewish scholar. He was researching, and writing a book on the Spanish Inquisition. We talked for hours about his findings.

Have you ever wondered why Columbus sailed in search of a new land in 1492? Queen Isabella and King Ferdinand had issued an edict of ejection regarding the Jews. It stated that every person of Jewish descent had to leave Spain or be executed.

Jewish businessmen went to Christopher Columbus, an Italian Jew, and pledged to finance his efforts to discover a new land. They purchased the ships that carried Columbus across the ocean to the shores of what would become America.

In 1776, when the 13 Colonies were fighting the British during the American Revolution, the colonial soldiers were poorly armed, starving to death, and on the verge of defeat. A Jewish banker from Philadelphia, Hyman Solomon, went to the Jews in America and Europe, and gathered a gift of one million dollars. He gave the money to George Washington to buy clothes and arms to outfit the American troops. Life, liberty, and the pursuit of happiness were born on American soil as a result of that gift.

To show his appreciation, George Washington had the engravers of the U.S. one dollar bill include a memorial to the Jewish people over the head of the American eagle. Look closely. You will find 13 stars of the Mogen David, the Star of Israel. Around that star is the cloudburst of the glory in the tabernacle. Our God-fearing President George Washington decreed that there must be a memorial to the Jewish people for the contributions they made to further this nation.

America has been blessed because she has blessed the nation of Israel (Genesis 12:1-3). But America is in danger of moving away from the place of blessing to the place of cursing. The land-for-peace deals of recent years have placed Israel and the Jewish people in grave danger. To weaken Israel is to risk the peace of the world, for the road to world peace runs through Israel. Israel is the firewall between America and the anti-Semitic Islamic nations. America's ability to win the war on terrorism will be directly related to America's willingness to support Israel in winning the war against terrorism. Israel is the only power that restrains Islamic terrorism from the West. Jews are dying so that

Christians can live. Terrorists consider America a Christian nation. They do not hate America because of Israel; they hate Israel because of America. They refer to America as the Great Satan, and Israel as the Little Satan.

Some may say, "I don't need to reach out to the suffering House of Israel. Why, the Bible says there will be wars and rumors of wars over there, until the Messiah comes. It's all part of prophecy." This Scripture is taken from Matthew 24:6. It refers to the entire world. As a matter of fact, there have only been approximately 268 years of peace on this planet in the last 6,000 years. This is despite the fact that some 8,000 peace treaties have been signed. However, there have also been some amazing revivals during that time!

To simply say that there is no need to pray and support the Jewish people, my friend, is anti-Semitic nonsense. It is to say to Nehemiah, Esther, and even our Lord that they were wrong to pray and reach out in love to the House of Israel. There are hundreds of examples of prophets, priests and kings who chose to light a candle rather than curse the darkness. Jesus is our perfect example. He fed the hungry. He gave water to the thirsty. He healed the sick. And yet, He prophesied that the Temple would be torn down, and Jerusalem left in shambles.

The Bible says the same thing about the entire

world in 2 Timothy 3:1:

*"But know this, that in the last days per-
ilous times will come."*

Matthew 24:6-8:

*"And you will hear of wars and rumors of
wars. See that you are not troubled; for all these
things must come to pass, but the end is not yet.
For nation will rise against nation, and kingdom
against kingdom. And there will be famines,
pestilences, and earthquakes in various places.
All these are the beginning of sorrows."*

If we are to do nothing, then why do we do
everything in our power to help hurting people in
our own country?

The Apostle Paul warned Christians not to act
arrogantly against the physical descendants of
Jacob, even though most had been "blinded" to the
fact that Jesus is their long-promised Messiah. However, arrogance would have been welcomed in comparison to the ugly hatred and deadly violence that
was frequently aimed at the Jewish people in the
name of Christ. This alone should be reason enough
for contemporary Christians to humbly support the
Jewish people in their difficult struggle to rebuild
their ancient homeland in the hostile Middle East.

7. Because **God Says** We are to **Comfort Israel**

(Isaiah 40:1)

"Comfort ye, comfort ye my people saith your God. Speak ye comfortably to Jerusalem…"
(Isaiah 40:1-2, KJV).

This prophetic word is a God-given mandate to Christians to offer comfort, encouragement, and emotional and financial support to the suffering House of Israel. If this Scripture is not for Christians then for whom? Nation after nation has turned its back on the Jewish people.

God said, *"Whom shall I send, and who will go for us?"* Isaiah cried out, "Here am I; send me." The Lord is saying, one million praying Christians can win the war that is being fought right now in the Bible land. Wake up, the mighty men; wake up, the mighty women! Wake up the Esthers and Nehemiahs! *"But the people that do know their God shall be strong, and do exploits"* (Daniel 11:32, KJV).

We as Christians are called to show God's love to the suffering House of Israel as Corrie ten Boom did. 25 years ago in September of 1986, I went to Holland, purchased and restored the ten Boom clock shop. It was opened as a witness of the love of Christians for the Jewish people. Corrie and her family saved 800 Jewish lives! As the Apostle Paul said, *"concerning the election they are beloved for the sake of the fathers. For the gifts and the calling of God are irrevocable*" (Romans 11:28-29).

If Christians who are able to bless the house of Israel withhold that blessing, especially by not reaching out toward those who are suffering from terrorist attacks such as the ones that happened during the Holocaust, how will Jews ever know that real Christians are different than those who name His name but kill Jews? To comfort the house of Israel is our duty, and our privilege.

"But when He saw the multitudes (the Jews), He was moved with compassion for them, because they were weary and scattered, like sheep having no shepherd" (Matthew 9:36)

"But thou, O LORD, shalt endure forever; and thy remembrance unto all generations. Thou shalt arise, and have mercy upon Zion: for the time to favour her, yea, the set time, is come" (Psalm 102:12-13, KJV).

8. Because **God Says** His Gifts and Calls to Israel Have not Been Revoked

"Can a woman forget her sucking child, that she should not have compassion on the son of her womb? Yea, they may forget, yet will I not forget thee" (Isaiah 49:15, KJV).

"Boast not against the branches. But if thou boast, thou bearest not the root, but the root thee. Thou wilt say then, The branches were broken off, that I might be grafted in. Well; because of unbelief they were broken off, and thou standest by faith. Be not highminded, but fear" (Romans 11:18-20, KJV).

"God has not cast away His people whom he foreknew" (Romans 11:2).

I recently spent an afternoon in Jerusalem with Russian Jews who came to Israel as refugees. One of the elderly Jewish ladies who had just buried her second son as a result of a terrorist attack asked, "Why are the Christians killing us? I fled Russia to get away from the Russian Orthodox Christians that hated us, only to run right into American Christians who have divided our land and forced the terrorists on us." The House of Israel has fallen among robbers who have not only stolen their land but their lives.

Where is the Good Samaritan? *"He who touches you (Israel) touches the apple of his (God's) eye"*

(Zechariah 2:8). Heed the words of Jesus as He spoke concerning the House of Israel:

> *"For I was an hungered, and ye gave me no meat: I was thirsty, and ye gave me no drink: I was a stranger, and ye took me not in: naked, and ye clothed me not: sick, and in prison, and ye visited me not. Then shall they also answer him, saying, Lord, when saw we thee an hungered, or athirst, or a stranger, or naked, or sick, or in prison, and did not minister unto thee? Then shall he answer them, saying, Verily I say unto you, **Inasmuch as ye did it not to one of the least of these, ye did it not to me.**"* (Matthew 25:42-45, KJV).

In the above Scriptures, our Lord was referring to the Jews in Israel, His earthly seed. This Scripture means just what it says.

The truth is that the Jews were totally rejected during the Holocaust, and this was the response by the average Christian to their cries. May it not be the response today as a similar holocaust is taking place.

> *"I say then, Hath God cast away his people? God forbid. For I also am an Israelite, of the seed of Abraham, of the tribe of Benjamin. God hath not cast away his people which he foreknew"* (Romans 11:1-2, KJV).

> *"Who are Israelites; to whom pertaineth the adoption, and the glory, and the covenants, and*

the giving of the law, and the service of God, and the promises; Whose are the fathers, and of whom as concerning the flesh Christ came, who is over all, God blessed for ever. Amen" (Romans 9:4-5, KJV).

"James, a servant of God and of the Lord Jesus Christ, to the twelve tribes which are scattered abroad, greeting" (James 1:1, KJV).

If all the promises were revoked, then why did Paul not know it? Or James?

"Give none offence, neither to the Jews, nor to the Gentiles, nor to the Church of God" (1 Corinthians 10:32, KJV).

God will never forsake His Chosen People.

"For Israel hath not been forsaken, nor Judah of his God, of the LORD of hosts, though their land was filled with sin against the Holy One of Israel" (Jeremiah 51:5, KJV).

And if all the promises were revoked, why didn't John the Revelator know it? And why didn't our Lord and Savior who gave this revelation to John know it? You cannot read the book of Revelation and not be aware of Israel from the 7th through the 21st chapters. Revelation 7:2-8 speaks of the 12 tribes. Revelation 21:12 again speaks of the 12 tribes. Israel is, and will always be, God's Miracle Nation.

Some like to deny their responsibility, saying the Jews are blind. But the Word says, *"you shall see*

Me no more till you say, 'Blessed is He who comes in the name of the Lord!'" (Matthew 23:39). You cannot say you have been a blessing until you have been a blessing. When so-called Christians have murdered six million Jews in our lifetime, how can we expect Jewish people to listen to our message, while we still turn our backs on their pain?

There is a need for repentance. If a person comes in your name, kills another person and the family thinks you did it, don't you have an obligation to go to them and express your deep sorrow? Don't you think you should do all you can to heal the hurt?

Great numbers of real Christians did nothing to help during the Holocaust. They were silent. If you were Jewish, how would you feel when Christians sing in their churches about Jews in the Bible (Moses, David, Jesus), and talk about future Jews (144,000 in the book of Revelation), but do nothing to reach out in love to living Jews? What about when Christians remained silent as America forced Israel to give the world's most infamous terrorist organization, the PLO and its leaders, part of the Holy Land that would be used as a base to commit almost 10,000 terrorist attacks upon innocent Jews?

In 1997, I wrote the following article, *"Where's the Outrage?"* for *The Wall Street Journal*. It deals with the treatment of Arabs under Arafat's leadership.

Conditions have worsened since this article was printed.

On May 31, Ali Jamhour, a resident of a refugee camp east of Jerusalem, was found shot to death after he'd been questioned by Yasser Arafat's security forces about allegedly brokering land sales to Jewish Israelis. Jamhour was the third Palestinian land dealer killed after a Muslim cleric urged the killing of any Palestinian who'd sold land to Israelis; all were executed gangland-style by a bullet to the head. On June 1, Israeli police foiled the kidnapping of a fourth broker, in the process of uncovering evidence that high-ranking Palestinian officials are behind the murders.

While U.S. officials have deplored the killings, the White House has so far been strangely reticent in condemning the Palestinian Authority. Let Israel open a new exit to an old tunnel, or start construction on a new neighborhood in Jerusalem, and President Clinton immediately summons Prime Minister Netanyahu to Washington for a one-on-one session of diplomatic arm-twisting. So why doesn't Mr. Clinton yank Yasser Arafat by the lapels of his dictator-style military uniform, and explain to him that you cannot make peace through murder?

The answer is that the U.S. like most of the world, follows a double standard when it comes to Israeli-Arab conflicts. It's OK to vilify Israel for any act that might appear to be an exercise of sovereignty, yet each Palestin-

ian violation of the peace agreement receives no more than a wink.

It is one thing to forbid the sale of land to foreigners. A number of countries, particularly small countries surrounded by hostile neighbors, do the same; Israel itself has restricted selling land to Arabs. It is another thing, however, to kill those who violate the real estate restrictions. Imagine if Israel has announced it would impose the death penalty on anyone who sold land to Arabs. That would be front-page news around the world, and the U.S. President would issue a strongly-worded statement taking Israel to task for such an outrage. A White House summit would be scheduled, and the U.N. would instantly pass a resolution condemning Israel.

Yet when the Palestinian Authority continually made such a pronouncement and bodies started piling up, it took two weeks for any Clinton administration official to go on the record condemning the policy. It took longer still for the story to appear on the nightly news, and even then reporters passed along, without comment, the Palestinian's stock attempt to shift the blame. Perhaps the Israelis themselves were responsible, they suggested.

Israeli Prime Minister Benjamin Netanyahu, by contrast, has taken swift action. When Israeli intelligence turned up a Palestinian Authority hit list of 16 land dealers that included the names of the three already killed, Mr. Netanyahu called an emergency security session. The Netanyahu administration authorized the installation of alarm systems in the brokers' homes and increased police patrols in their neighborhoods.

Mr. Netanyahu also authorized an arrest warrant for a senior Palestinian official implicated in the land dealer executions. Israel security says it's established that the murders were carried out with the participation, as well as the approval of the Palestinian Authority. When Israel police foiled the June 1 kidnapping attempt, six armed men were arrested as they tried to flee to Ramallah, a Palestinian-controlled town just north of Jerusalem. Four of the would-be kidnappers were members of the Palestinian Authority security services. During the chase, the suspects ditched several weapons, one of which turned out to be the weapon used in two of the recent murders.

Such violence "goes against the grain of everything we expect the Palestinians to do to achieve peace between us," Mr. Netanyahu told Israeli radio.

Finally, Mr. Arafat responded—by telling a press conference that the Palestinian Authority had not authorized these murders and that he denounces terrorism. Within 24 hours, however, liberal Arutz Sheva radio in Israel reported, "The PA is continuing its efforts against Arabs suspected of selling land to Jews. It has abducted another 12 such persons, including some Israeli citizens."

Senator Jesse Helms, chairman of the Senate Foreign Relations Committee, and Rep. Benjamin Gilman, chairman of the House International Relations Committee, have announced they will oppose any further aid to the

Palestinians until they revoke their call to kill Arabs who sell land to Jews. It's time for President Clinton to do the same. Otherwise, Yasser Arafat and his deputized terrorists will be getting away with murder."

Restoration to the Promised Land

In light of the Biblical evidence presented until now, we must conclude that Christians have a God-given mandate to honor the Jewish people, wherever they are. But how does this connect to modern Israel? Many Christians seem happy enough to salute Jewish neighbors living alongside them in largely Gentile lands, but are indifferent or even hostile to the proposition that we also have a duty to support the controversial Jewish State of Israel. Some Believers bristle at the mere suggestion that God has anything to do with Israel's amazing restoration in our era.

Centuries before the Jewish people first were forced into foreign captivity, God revealed that they would be expelled from their covenant land due to sin. But He also promised to eventually restore them to the Promised Land. This prophecy came via Moses—whose parents came from the tribe of Levi—while he was in the process of boldly leading the children of Israel from the bondage of Egypt into

Canaan:

> "*That the Lord your God will bring you back from captivity, and have compassion on you, and gather you again from all the nations where the Lord your God has scattered you*" (Deuteronomy 30:3).

This prophecy could be speaking of the return of the Jewish people from Assyrian and Babylonian captivity hundreds of years before the time of Christ. Yet the ancient Hebrew prophets also foretold that Israel's loving God would restore His people to their Promised Land in the Last Days of history, just before Messiah begins His reign in Jerusalem. This implies that the Jews would be exiled two times from their beloved homeland, which is exactly what has taken place in history.

The prophets also foretold that the final Jewish ingathering would be from all over the globe, unlike the first return from lands directly to the east of Israel. It would be a permanent return, meaning no additional exiles would follow. Most significantly, it would end with the spiritual revival that King Solomon prophesied in 2 Chronicles 7:14.

There are many prophetic Scriptures about this important topic in the Bible—far too many to quote in this small booklet. But let's take a look at a few of them:

> "*I will bring back the captives of My people*

Israel; They shall build the waste cities and inhabit them; They shall plant vineyards and drink wine from them; They shall also make gardens and eat fruit from them. I will plant them in their land, And no longer shall they be pulled up From the land I have given them,' Says the Lord your God" (Amos 9:14-15).

"'For behold, the days are coming,' says the Lord, 'that I will bring back from captivity My people Israel and Judah,' says the Lord. 'And I will cause them to return to the land that I gave to their fathers, and they shall possess it.'" (Jeremiah 30:3).

"'Thus says the Lord God: "When I have gathered the house of Israel from the peoples among whom they are scattered, and am hallowed in them in the sight of the Gentiles, then they will dwell in their own land which I gave to My servant Jacob. And they will dwell safely there, build houses, and plant vineyards; yes, they will dwell securely, when I execute judgments on all those around them who despise them. Then they shall know that I am the Lord their God"'" (Ezekiel 28:25-26).

"He will set up a banner for the nations, And will assemble the outcasts of Israel, And gather together the dispersed of Judah From the four corners of the earth" (Isaiah 11:12).

"For I will take you from among the nations, gather you out of all countries, and bring you into your own land" (Ezekiel 36:24).

"And I will cause the captives of Judah and the captives of Israel to return, and will rebuild those places as at the first. I will cleanse them from all their iniquity by which they have sinned against Me, and I will pardon all their iniquities by which they have sinned and by which they have transgressed against Me" (Jeremiah 33:7-8).

The Hebrew prophets also revealed that the full ingathering of the scattered Jewish people would only be completed when the Messiah came to earth. In other words, some Jews will still be living outside of Israel during the end of this age. However, this does not lessen or negate the fact that a large-scale return has been occurring in our day. In fact, nearly half the Jews on Earth have now returned to their biblical Promised Land. Christians around the world should be exuberant supporters of this prophesied restoration, for it confirms that the God of Israel exists, that He holds the future in His capable hands, that He is a covenant-keeping Lord, and that He is a merciful God who forgives the sins of His people.

Many Christians ask me, "How do I know if my church is a Bible-believing church that doesn't teach replacement theology, progressive dispensationalism, or supersessionism?"

Ask yourself some questions:

1. Does my church pray for the Jewish people, the peace of Jerusalem and Israel?
2. Does my church give offerings of compassion to comfort them?
3. Does my church preach on Israel and its Biblical significance?
4. Does my church take tours to Israel?
5. Is there an Israeli flag in my church?
6. Does my church teach on the significance of the Church's Jewish roots?
7. Does my church have a Night to Honor Israel or a Jerusalem Prayer Summit annually?
8. Does my church ever preach against replacement theology, progressive dispensationalism, or supersessionism?

If the answer to these questions is "No," then you may be a member of a church that refuses to believe the Bible, and rejects God's Eternal promises to the House of Israel. If your church seems powerless, and appears not to be blessed by God, perhaps this is the reason.

Israel is a Miracle Nation because of its formation; and

when we stand with Israel, we are standing with God's prophetic plan.

We must be part of God's dream and His team and support Israel and the Jewish people. Their existence and the rebirth of Israel is a miracle. As Christians, we believe in miracles. The resurrection of our Lord was the greatest miracle. If He can live again, it is no problem at all for Him to restore the Nation of Israel.

Israel was not born in 1948. It was born in the heart of God and revealed to Abraham many years before the birth of Isaac. God made a blood covenant with Abraham that the land of Canaan would be given to Abraham's seed through Isaac (Genesis 15:18). As part of that vision, God told Abraham that for 400 years his seed would be strangers in a land that did not belong to them (Genesis 15:13). The seed of Abraham from Isaac spent 400 years in Egypt before Moses led them out, and Israel, the nation, was born.

"Who has heard such a thing? Who has seen such things? Shall the earth be made to give birth in one day? Or shall a nation be born at once? For as soon as Zion was in labor, She gave birth to her children" (Isaiah 66:8).

Enduring Covenant People

Unique as this religious centrality is, there is one reason above all others why committed Christians must stand with Israel: The God of the Universe, the God that we worship, has chosen to make an *everlasting* covenant with the physical descendents of Abraham, Isaac, and Jacob—the Jewish people.

The word "everlasting" has nothing temporary or conditional about it. It clearly means, "lasting forever." And although Jews are found today in North and South America, Australia, Russia, Europe, many parts of Africa, and virtually every other continent on earth, their historic spiritual and physical center was, and always will be, the Promised Land of Israel.

God's eternal covenant with the descendents of Abraham featured the promise to give them the land of Israel as an everlasting possession. This is recorded in the very first book of the Bible, Genesis, in chapter 17:

> *"When Abram was ninety-nine years old, the Lord appeared to Abram and said to him, 'I am Almighty God; walk before Me and be blameless. And I will make My covenant between Me and you, and will multiply you exceedingly.' Then Abram fell on his face, and God talked with him, saying: 'As for Me, behold,*

My covenant is with you, and you shall be a father of many nations. No longer shall your name be called Abram, but your name shall be Abraham; for I have made you a father of many nations. I will make you exceedingly fruitful; and I will make nations of you, and kings shall come from you. And I will establish My covenant between Me and you and your descendants after you in their generations, for an everlasting covenant, to be God to you and your descendants after you. Also I give to you and your descendants after you the land in which you are a stranger, all the land of Canaan, as an everlasting possession; and I will be their God'" (Genesis 17:1-8).

It is true God reveals in these verses that many peoples will eventually emerge out of Abraham's loins, and so it has been. The Arabs, scattered in over 20 countries throughout the Middle East and North Africa, trace their ancestry to the Biblical patriarch who traveled to Canaan at God's command from the town of Ur in Chaldea. Their lineage comes through Abraham's first-born son, Ishmael. However, the Scriptures go on to reveal that the special, eternal land covenant, and others, will come through the line of Isaac, Jacob, and his 12 sons— the forefathers of the modern Jewish people. This is summarized in Psalm 105, verses 8 through 11:

"He remembers His covenant forever, The word which He commanded, for a thousand generations, The covenant which He made with Abraham, And His oath to Isaac, And confirmed it to Jacob for a statute, To Israel as an everlasting covenant, Saying, 'To you I will give the land of Canaan As the allotment of your inheritance.'"

The belief that God has revoked His solemn land covenant with the Jewish people, due to their sin and rebellion against Him, is widespread in the Church today. It is certainly a fact that living peacefully in the land was conditional on obedience to God's holy law. Jacob's offspring were warned that they would be removed from the land if they disobeyed God's commands. But the Bible also foretells that a Jewish remnant would be restored to the Promised Land after a worldwide exile, as is wonderfully occurring in our day.

9. Because **God Almighty** has Preserved Israel!

"Behold, He who keeps Israel Shall neither slumber nor sleep. The Lord is your keeper; The Lord is your shade at your right hand. The sun shall not strike you by day, Nor the moon by night. The Lord shall preserve you from all evil; He shall preserve your soul. The Lord shall preserve your going out and your coming in From this time forth, and even forevermore" (Psalm 121:4-8).

God has not permitted any power to exterminate the Jewish people, although no race has been pursued more throughout history. Many attempts have been made to annihilate the Jews, but such attempts have ended in utter failure, defeat, and humiliation.

Let's look at Pharaoh. *"So Pharaoh commanded all his people, saying, 'Every son who is born you shall cast into the river, and every daughter you shall save alive.'"* (Exodus 1:22). The very nation that ordered the casting of every Hebrew male child into the river had its **own** army thrown into the Red Sea when Moses brought the Children of Israel out of Egypt!

Esther is another great example. During the reign of King Ahasuerus, Haman decided to destroy the Jews, but instead **he** was hanged on the gallows that he had prepared for Mordecai, the Jew (Esther 7:10).

Satan's attempt to annihilate the Jews during World War II is another major example. Hitler declared they were not the Chosen People, that the Aryan race was, and that he would resolve the "Jewish problem." Hitler is even quoted as saying,

"There is no room for two chosen people." He murdered six million Jews in concentration camps. At the end of the war, Germany was divided, and Hitler committed suicide. On the other hand, and at almost the same time, Israel was reborn and God's people were preserved.

During World War II, there were five strategic incidents where the Allies could, and should have lost the war. Because of the supernatural intervention of God, they did not. The reason, I believe, was because of Germany's stance against the Jewish people. If the nations that come against Israel do not repent, Almighty God will once again bring judgment upon those nations.

The preservation of Israel through all of its suffering, wars and afflictions over the centuries is further evidence that Israel is God's miracle nation. Why have the Jews been hated so? Because Satan's only adversary would come through the Jews: The Messiah. And ultimately that Messiah would destroy the powers of Satan.

"And he gathered them together to the place called in Hebrew, Armageddon" (Revelation 16:16).

"On that day his feet will stand on the Mount of Olives, east of Jerusalem" (Zechariah 14:4, NIV).

"How you are fallen from heaven, O

Lucifer, son of the morning! How you are cut down to the ground, You who weakened the nations! For you have said in your heart: 'I will ascend into heaven, I will exalt my throne above the stars of God; I will also sit on the mount of the congregation On the farthest sides of the north; I will ascend above the heights of the clouds, I will be like the Most High.' Yet you shall be brought down to Sheol, To the lowest depths of the Pit." (Isaiah 14:12-15).

Eternal Land **Covenant**

The happy fact is that our God is a covenant-keeping God. He remains faithful even when we are faithless (2 Timothy 2:13). It is He who has sovereignly decided to preserve the Jewish people as a separate, identifiable people before Him until the end of time, and then to restore them to their Biblical homeland. These truths are revealed in several Scriptures. That they would remain on Earth until the end of time as a distinct people group is foretold in Jeremiah, Chapter 31:

"Thus says the Lord, Who gives the sun for a light by day, The ordinances of the moon and the stars for a light by night, Who disturbs the sea, And its waves roar (The Lord of hosts is His name): 'If those ordinances depart From before

Me, says the Lord, Then the seed of Israel shall also cease From being a nation before Me forever.'" (Jeremiah 31:35-36).

Many Bible teachers and denominations argue that Jewish sin, and particularly the general rejection of Jesus as their Messiah nearly 2,000 years ago, was more than enough reason for God to erase the "everlasting" land promise. But the next verse makes crystal clear that the God of Abraham has no intention of ever forsaking His special covenant with Jacob's children, despite their many failures:

"'I will direct their work in truth, And will make with them an everlasting covenant. Their descendants shall be known among the Gentiles, And their offspring among the people. All who see them shall acknowledge them, That they are the posterity whom the Lord has blessed'" (Isaiah 61:8-9).

When I founded the National Prayer Breakfast in Honor of Israel in 1982, Senator Billy Armstrong placed my message in the *Congressional Record*. It states clearly why Americans must stand with Israel.

CONGRESSIONAL RECORD COPY
Washington, D.C., Tuesday, March 16, 1982

"Proclamation of Blessing"

As Bible-believing Americans, we believe there exists an iron-clad bond between the State of Israel and the United States. We believe that bond to be a moral imperative.

Representing the vast majority of evangelicals in the United States, we have gathered together at this National Prayer Breakfast to reaffirm our support and prayers, that this bond not be weakened or diminished

We agree with the sentiments of our President:
'That a secure, strong Israel is in America's self-interest. Israel is a major strategic asset to America. Israel is not a client, but a very reliable friend. To weaken Israel is to destabilize the Middle East and risk the peace of the world, for the road to world peace runs through the Middle East.'

We support Israel's right to their land spiritually and legally. History records that God deals with nations in accordance with how these nations deal with Israel. We rejoice that here in America, for 206 years {now 235 years}, we have been committed to the Jewish people. The Jewish people have found refuge here; they have found a people who love them; and we can take pride in saying that Israel is not an exclusively Jewish issue.

Bible-believing evangelicals consider the support of Israel a Biblical mandate. Regardless of contrary opinion, we do not believe Israel has to offer an excuse for its existence. Israel lives today as a right—a right that has been hallowed by the Bible, by history, by sacrifice, by prayer, *and by the yearning for peace!*

> *"'I will bring back the captives of My people
> Israel; They shall build the waste cities and
> inhabit them; They shall plant vineyards and
> drink wine from them; They shall also make gar-
> dens and eat fruit from them. I will plant them
> in their land, And no longer shall they be pulled
> up From the land I have given them,' Says the
> Lord your God"* (Amos 9:14-15).

*We believe one of the reasons America has been
blessed over the years is because we have stood with
Israel. This promise is taken from Genesis 12:3, "I will
bless them that bless thee." So, for Biblical reasons first
and foremost, we support the State of Israel. For humanitarian reasons, we support the Jewish people. For historical reasons, believing that Palestine belongs to the Jewish
people, we support the State of Israel. For legal reasons,
dating back to 1948, and even further to the establishment of the British Mandate, we believe the land of Palestine belongs to the Jewish people.*

*Israel and the United States are not separate and dis-
tinct—we are one. We share common ideals and common
democracy. What unites us across the ocean, and brings
Jew and Christian together, is the recognition that Israel
is a nation that is a manifestation of what America was
and is.*

*America has a strong interest in the Middle East. We
affirm our belief that the nation of Israel is the key to that*

interest because of our common bonds, our common values, our common belief in social justice, and the Godly principles on which our two countries were founded.

In affirmation of these beliefs, we hereby set our hands this 10th day of February, 1982.

God calls the land of Israel, "My Land" (Ezekiel 38:16), and He gave it to Israel by a blood covenant that cannot be changed. God has assigned the land of Israel to the children of Israel. God has never cancelled what He assigned.

Jews returning to Israel is a fulfillment of Prophecy.

God said that Israel would be scattered among the heathen and they were. But He also said they would be re-gathered and they have been.

"He will set up a banner for the nations, And will assemble the outcasts of Israel, And gather together the dispersed of Judah From the four corners of the earth" (Isaiah 11:12)

"I will bring back the captives of My people Israel" (Amos 9:14)

"For I will take you from among the nations, gather you out of all countries, and bring you into your own land" (Ezekiel 36:24).

"I will bring them back to this place, and I will cause them to dwell safely" (Jeremiah 32:37).

"I will plant them in their land, And no longer shall they be pulled up From the land I have given them" (Amos 9:15).

"'I will say to the north, "Give them up!" And to the south, "Do not keep them back!" Bring My sons from afar, And My daughters from the ends of the earth" (Isaiah 43:6)

"Thus says the Lord God: 'Behold, I will lift My hand in an oath to the nations, And set up My standard for the peoples; They shall bring your sons in their arms, And your daughters shall be carried on their shoulders" (Isaiah 49:22).

Corrie ten Boom believed this her entire life. Her grandfather, Willem ten Boom, founded a prayer meeting in Holland at the ten Boom clock shop in 1844. They prayed for the Jewish people that they might return to their land, according to Psalm 122:6. That prayer meeting lasted 100 years until they were taken to the Nazi death camps, where most of the ten Boom family gave their lives for saving Jewish people. As Chairman of the Corrie ten Boom House, I have resurrected this family prayer meeting tradition. It is now spreading all over the world. You can be part of it, too! (www.jerusalemprayerteam.org)

It is of great interest to notice that Isaiah predicted the people of Israel would return to their homeland by airplanes, hundreds of years before the invention of airplanes. *"Who are these who fly like a cloud, And like doves to their roosts?"* (Isaiah 60:8). He also predicted that they would return by ships:

> *"Surely the isles shall wait for me, and the ships of Tarshish first, to bring thy sons from far, their silver and their gold with them, unto the name of the LORD thy God, and to the Holy One of Israel, because he hath glorified thee"* (Isaiah 60:9, KJV).

The final restoration of the Jews to their homeland comes with a wonderful promise:

> *"And I will bring again the captivity of my people of Israel, and they shall build the waste cities, and inhabit them; and they shall plant vineyards, and drink the wine thereof: they shall also make gardens, and eat the fruit of them. And I will plant them upon their land, and they shall no more be pulled out of their land which I have given them, saith the LORD thy God"* (Amos 9:14-15, KJV).

10. Because God Says He Would Raise Up Intercessors!

"I have set watchmen upon thy walls, O Jerusalem, which shall never hold their peace day nor night: ye that make mention of the LORD, keep not silence, And give him no rest, till he establish, and till he make Jerusalem a praise in the earth" (Isaiah 62:6-7, KJV).

"Who hath heard such a thing? who hath seen such things? Shall the earth be made to bring forth in one day? or shall a nation be born at once? for as soon as Zion travailed, she brought forth her children. Shall I bring to the birth, and not cause to bring forth? saith the LORD: shall I cause to bring forth , and shut the womb? saith thy God. Rejoice ye with Jerusalem, and be glad with her, all ye that love her: rejoice for joy with her, all ye that mourn for her: That ye may suck, and be satisfied with the breasts of her consolations; that ye may milk out, and be delighted with the abundance of her glory. For thus saith the LORD, Behold, I will extend peace to her like a river, and the glory of the Gentiles like a flowing stream: then shall ye suck , ye shall be borne upon her sides, and be dandled upon her knees. As one whom his mother comforteth, so will I comfort you; and ye shall be comforted in Jerusalem" (Isaiah 66:8-13, KJV).

Nothing is more important to God than prayer. God will do nothing without prayer. The fuel that moves the engine of

humanity is prayer.

God has a purpose and a plan for our lives. The lives of our nation and the nation of Israel are dependent on prayer. His will and His blessings are bound up in prayer. Almighty God created the world, and He created the nation of Israel. His purposes and plans are more important than anything that man can do.

"Call unto me, and I will answer thee, and shew thee great and mighty things, which thou knowest not" (Jeremiah 33:3, KJV).

As Jeremiah prophesied to the Jewish people during their captivity in Babylon, he was given this promise. The Jews were ultimately delivered from captivity, and revival came to Israel.

"Thus saith the LORD, the Holy One of Israel, and his Maker, Ask me of things to come concerning my sons, and concerning the work of my hands command ye me" (Isaiah 45:11, KJV).

God takes prayer so seriously that He even says that we can *"command Him"* (Isaiah 45:11). Although this sounds like heresy, it is nonetheless true.

Daniel in Babylon (Iraq) refused to obey the decree of the king. The king had decreed that no one could ask any petition of any God or man for 30 days. But Daniel, who prayed three times a day (Daniel 6:1-23), continued to pray just as he had done before the decree. The God that Daniel was honoring honored Daniel and shut the mouth of the lion in the lion's den. Daniel's prayers prevailed in the midst of Israel's captivity in Babylon.

> *"For thus saith the LORD, That after seventy years be accomplished at Babylon I will visit you, and perform my good word toward you, in causing you to return to this place. For I know the thoughts that I think toward you, saith the LORD, thoughts of peace, and not of evil, to give you an expected end. Then shall ye call upon me, **and ye shall go and pray unto me, and I will hearken unto you.** And ye shall seek me, and find me, when ye shall search for me with all your heart. And I will be found of you, saith the LORD: and I will turn away your captivity, **and I will gather you from all the nations**, and from all the places whither I have driven you, saith the LORD; and I will bring you again into the place whence I caused you to be carried away captive"* (Jeremiah 29:10-14, KJV).

Abraham is a striking example of the power of prayer. He interceded for Sodom for Lot's sake and God delayed judgment. God would have even spared Sodom for ten righteous souls (Genesis 18:20-33). He thought surely Lot and his wife, his daughters, his sons and sons-in-law would be righteous and total more than ten.

Abraham was a praying man. Wherever he pitched his tent and camped for a season with his household, there he erected an altar of sacrifice and of prayer. In another example, God said to Abimelech, Abraham *"is a prophet, and he shall pray for thee, and thou shalt live"* (Genesis 20:7, KJV). God heard Abraham's prayers, and He will hear ours. That's why He wants us to be part of His Team and His Dream.

Moses prayed for 40 days for Israel. The result of his prayers was a mighty deliverance for the nation of Israel. God's movement to bring Israel from bondage had its inception in prayer (Exodus 2:23-25; 3:9).

September 11th was a visit from hell, planned in hell by demon spirits. The terrorist holocaust in Israel is also a result of the same spiritual powers. These powers cannot be defeated without prayer. Praying saints are God's agents to carry out His will on earth. America is helpless without prayer, as is Israel. **If Jesus said that He could do nothing without prayer, then we surely cannot hope to accomplish anything of eternal significance without prayer.**

A Christian that refuses to pray is like a swimmer that refuses to get in the water. All the talking in the world of how much we know about swimming will only bring those we are trying to influence to laughter. For a Christian, to refuse to make prayer the number one priority is like saying to Al Qaeda, "We refuse to fight; you win!" Our weapons of war and our Commander in Chief is waiting to win the Battle, we only need to speak the Word.

"Then one of the seraphim flew to me, having in his hand a live coal which he had taken with the tongs from the altar. And he touched my mouth with it, and said: 'Behold, this has touched your lips; Your iniquity is taken away, And your sin purged'" (Isaiah 6:6-7).

Darkness flees when we pray! Demons tremble when we pray. Heaven moves when we pray, and angels receive assignment when we pray. Prayer affects three realms: The Divine, the Angelic, and the Human. Without it, demons rule uncontested (Ephesians 6).

Hannah's petition for a son (1 Samuel 1:11) began a great prayer movement for God in Israel. Hannah's prayers birthed Samuel the Prophet who would anoint a shepherd boy to become the king of Israel and rule over the City of David. Samuel was a man of prayer. He stood before the people on one occasion and said, *"far be it from me that I should sin against the Lord in ceasing to pray for you"* (1 Samuel 12:23).

We cannot make contact with God without prayer. If we don't make contact with God, no matter how sincere our intentions are, we will not see a change in the circumstances of life.

When King Solomon prayed at the dedication of the Temple, God showed up with great power and revealed His plan to Solomon (2 Chronicles 7:12-15). He called unto God in prayer and Jehovah was there. *"Then you shall call, and the Lord will answer; You shall cry, and He will say, 'Here I am'"* (Isaiah 58:9). King Solomon prophesied that a national revival was coming to Israel. It has not happened yet; and it can only come through the power of prayer. You and I can usher in that revival through prayer.

Hezekiah was another example of God's response to prayer and repentance. During a dark hour of Israel's history, the Assyrians demanded heavy tribute from the king. In response, Hezekiah stripped the Temple of its gold and silver in order to meet the demand. Still that was not enough. The Assyrians mounted an attack against the city. Hezekiah bowed before God, and prayed. God responded with an amazing victory! He sent a plague that killed 185,000 Assyrian soldiers.

In great gratitude for God's mercy, Hezekiah cleansed, repaired, and reopened the Temple of God. Worship to Jehovah was restored. Daily sacrifices were resumed. The Passover Feast was celebrated by the nation.

"If My people who are called by My name will humble themselves, and pray and seek My face, and turn from their wicked ways, then I will hear from heaven, and will forgive their sin and heal their land" (2 Chronicles 7:14).

God has watchmen on the wall. We call them Esthers and Nehemiahs…members of the Jerusalem Prayer Team…people like Corrie ten Boom, and hopefully, people like you.

The world has been scratching its head trying to find an answer to the crisis in the Bible land. That answer is in your hands and mine.

"You do not have because you do not ask" (James 4:2).

"So I say to you, ask, and it will be given to you; seek, and you will find; knock, and it will be opened to you. For everyone who asks receives, and he who seeks finds, and to him who knocks it will be opened" (Luke 11:9-10).

You may be like Jonah. He did everything but pray. He knew what God wanted him to do, but kept resisting. Jonah fled, and ended up in the belly of a big fish. There he cried out to God against whom he had sinned. God intervened and caused the fish to vomit Jonah out onto dry land. Even the fish of the sea are subject to the power of prayer. When those in Nineveh saw this stinking, praying prophet, they repented quickly and God sent revival.

"Then another angel, having a golden censer, came and stood at the altar. He was given much incense, that he should offer it with the prayers of all the saints upon the golden altar which was before the throne. And the smoke of the incense, with the prayers of the saints, ascended before God from the angel's hand. Then the angel took the censer, filled it with fire from the altar, and threw it to the earth. And there were noises, thunderings, lightnings, and an earthquake" (Revelation 8:3-5).

Conclusion

"For if the Gentiles have been partakers of their spiritual things, their duty is also to minister to them in material things" (Romans 15:27).

Stand with Israel!

If the revealed will of God and the record of history mean anything to followers of the Jewish Messiah—as they must—we can only conclude that Christians have a heaven-ordained duty to love and support the Jewish people in every possible way. More than a duty, we should consider it our great privilege to bless the people who have blessed us; especially by being the channels through which our sacred Bible and our precious salvation have come to us.

Jesus Himself said that the Son of Man will pass judgment on the nations when He comes to rule on His glorious throne as King of Kings (Matthew 25:31). He went on to reveal that the main criteria for judgment would be how Gentiles treated His brothers (25:40). Of course, all of us who are faithful followers of the Great Shepherd are the Lord's spiritual brethren. But Jesus' Jewish kin will always be His basic family stock, and thus His particular brethren. There is good reason to believe that these are the ones the Lord was referring to in the 25th chapter of Matthew.

Paul confirms that the Lord wants Christians to especially bless the Jewish people (Romans 15:26-27). Indeed, these Scriptures reveal that Jewish Believers in Jesus—who are once again greatly multiplying in our day—should be the direct recipients of financial blessings from Gentile Believers:

"For it pleased those from Macedonia and Achaia to make a certain contribution for the poor among the saints who are in Jerusalem. It pleased them indeed, and they are their debtors. For if the Gentiles have been partakers of their spiritual things, their duty is also to minister to them in material things."

Christians have been blessed beyond words by being grafted into the rich olive tree of Israel. Therefore, we must minister to the Jewish Believers in the Promised Land in many ways, but especially by actively supporting their right to live there. This is doubly important since widespread anti-Semitism has once again reared its ugly head in recent years.

My dear friend, Prime Minister Yitzhak Rabin was asked by President Clinton to take a "brave gamble." I appealed to Rabin in person and by letter not to believe that lie. My appeal was not heard by this beloved man.

This is the text of the letter that I sent to the Prime Minister:

Dear Prime Minister Rabin,

I just left the White House with a broken heart. I did not go to be a part of the Arafat celebration. I went as a representative of the 50 million evangelicals in America. My purpose for going, Mr. Prime Minister, was not to express support for Yasser Arafat, nor to get his auto-

graph, but to express support for Israel's Bible Lands.

I did not feel tears running down my face as many did at the White House. Nor did my heart pound from hyped-up media reports of an historic reconciliation with a man who ordered the murders of school children in Avivim, Ma'alot and Antwerp, of eleven Jewish athletes in Munich, Synagogue worshippers in Istanbul, a child and his pregnant mother in Alfeh Menashe, and a mother and her children on a bus in Jericho. This same man who ordered innocent Arabs in Nablus hanged by their chins on butcher's hooks until they died, ordered the bellies of pregnant Arab women split open before the eyes of their husbands, and the hands of Arab children chopped off while their parents watched...simply because these Arabs disagreed.

Mr. Prime Minister, how can the government of Israel commit itself to the withdrawal of armed forces from Gaza and Jericho and provide security for Israeli citizens in the West Negev and in southern Israel? How can the doors opening to the Palestinians, worldwide, into Jericho and Gaza, keep from escalating terrorism and a deepening of hostility? How will foreign international forces insure Israel's security? They didn't do it in Lebanon when the United Nation forces worked with the P.L.O. When the P.L.O. strikes Israel, it will be virtually impossible for Israel to retaliate with the U.N. or international forces in the way.

As evangelicals, we believe in peace and forgiveness.

Indeed, this is the Jewish year 5754 when your nation is in the midst of celebrating its Holy days. During this Holy season, there is a need for repentance, humbling ourselves and asking forgiveness by God Almighty, for any and all sins.

Mr. Prime Minister, the healing and reconciliation must happen in the human heart between Arab and Jew. The basis for it cannot be land nor cutting deals with a terrorist who has repented of nothing. God dearly loves the Arab people just as He loves your beloved people. The question is how will innocent children and even innocent civilians benefit by dealing with shrewd, demon-inspired terrorists and politicians who wish Israel no good...only their destruction. To think that the P.L.O. would take over the administrated territories that God Almighty gave to your beloved people, and that more than 120,000 settlers in these territories will be subject to the P.L.O. is beyond reason. Even if the army succeeds in protecting them against terrorists, no Jew will want to live at the mercy of a dictatorial P.L.O. regime, which will have control of land, water and services.

President Clinton has coined this..."a brave gamble." Mr. Prime Minister, one does not gamble with God's prophetic land nor His prophetic plan. Nebuchadnezzar tried that and lived to greatly regret it.

In my 13 meetings with Prime Minister Begin, we talked about building a bridge based upon mutual respect. My greatest fear, Mr. Prime Minister, is that there seems to be a bridge being built between Gaza and Jericho based upon destruction. Can you imagine America inviting a terrorist organization that had terrorized our country and killed our civilians like Arafat has yours to have a state in Virginia...just a few miles from our capital, Washington, D.C.? There is no question that Arafat demands a Palestinian state and not in Jericho and Gaza. He wants it all.

Prime Minister Rabin, we believe that God Almighty promised the land of Israel, in its entirety, to your people, and the promises of God's Word are non-negotiable.

On October 30, 1991, at the Middle East Peace Conference, I boldly confronted Secretary of State, James Baker, and said the following,

"Most of the times that our Presidents have run for election, they have always told us evangelicals that they were going to move the U.S. Embassy to Jerusalem. Obviously, every capital in the world is recognized as a capital, except Jerusalem. Why can't America recognize Jerusalem as Israel's capital as a gesture of peace? Secondly, we are moving our military presence into the Arab world for a sense of security, why can't we have a military presence in Israel to help its security? It has suffered so greatly...especially paying such a dear price during the Persian Gulf War."

You know Mr. Baker's response...

"These things must be determined by negotiations."

With whom shall God negotiate? One must be very

careful before one begins negotiating on Bible Lands without considering the God who gave these lands. If one determines that they are going to divide what God Almighty has given, then indeed, the judgment of God could very severely fall upon the head of that individual. Either God exists...or He doesn't. Either God's Word is true...or it isn't. If He does, and it is, then one must walk very softly.

At the 43rd Session of the U.N. General Assembly meeting in Geneva on December 13, 1988, Arafat made the statement...

"The only birth certificate for the establishment for the state of Israel is resolution 181 approved by the General Assembly on November 29, 1947."

"...the first and decisive resolution of our Palestine National Council was the proclamation of the establishment of the state of Palestine with the Holy City of Jerusalem-al-Quds ask-Shareef as its capital."

Arafat, on December 13, 1988, stated in his speech:

"I condemn terrorism in all its forms."

Only God knows the number of funerals you have had since 1988 when Arafat lied. Prime Minister Rabin, I have written six major books on your nation and hundreds of articles. I have worked very closely with, and have had eighteen meetings with your last four prime ministers. In the last two decades, when Israel has had a crisis, I have always been there. Based upon my experience and knowledge, I do not believe for a second that there is any intention of these players in the peace process, to respect Israel's rights. This is more Arab "rhetoric"... more as we say, "shuck and jive."

Mount Calvary, the Lord's Tomb, the Mount of Olives, the Via Dolorosa, the Garden of Gethsemane and even the Temple site where we believe the Messiah will come back to...are all part of East Jerusalem. We believe in our Bible that it will be in Jewish hands when our Messiah returns. To place it in the hands of an Arab P.L.O. State is paramount to ripping pages of prophecy right out of the Bible and shaking your fist in the face of God Almighty who gave you this land.

I see no indication that America's policy has changed, nor that Arafat's policies have changed. When three Palestinians are on trial for attempting to blow up the World Trade Center...when four graves were being dug in Jerusalem because of Palestinians killing Israelis while you were with Arafat at the White House, and when the very man who embraced Saddam Hussein and helped orchestrate a war not only to eliminate Kuwait but to hopefully destroy Israel, has repented of nothing...even refusing adamantly to denounce terrorism in his speech at the White House...I cannot understand why you would shake his hand.

Mr. Prime Minister, you and I met recently and I gave you copies of my specials that were seen by more than 23 million people in America, "Israel, America's Key to Survival," "Jerusalem, D.C. ," and "Let My People

Go." I brought my Bible. We discussed the prophecies of the Bible, and I prayed with you. I urged you to base your decisions on the Bible and not public opinion, because ultimately the blessings of God will be the determining factor upon which nations fall or rise. I have made the same appeal to your predecessors during the last two decades.

Twenty-three nations, which lifted their hands against your nation throughout history, have ceased to exist. But the people of the Book live on. Perseverance based upon faith in God and in His Word will outlast persecution.

I appeal to you to make your decisions based upon God's promise to your land. Israel was not created in 1948, and Jerusalem was not given to you in 1967. It was given by God Almighty 3,000 years ago through the father of your faith, Abraham. If the Bible is not to be considered the basis for your right to the land, then you may as well tell the people of Israel to pack their bags. Life will become so unbearable, the Jews will not want to move to Israel and great numbers there will move out because of the hell they are going through...like a great exodus. The world community will attempt to pressure Israel to give up every inch of land possible...making life absolutely unbearable for your beloved nation.

Prime Minister Rabin, this week I will address the entire nation of the former U.S.S.R. and all of its republics. I will be speaking to them for one hour, prime *time, from 7:00-8:00 p.m. on Moscow I, on September 26. This is a message that I spoke at the Kremlin Palace. With all of my heart, I believe that the one million Russian Jews coming to Israel is a fulfillment of prophecy. This prophetic exodus must continue, but it will not, based upon Arafat's present policies.*

On Monday, September 13, Yasser Arafat made his pledge and promise to America and Israel that he would accept Jericho and Gaza, but on Sunday, September 19, the P.L.O. Chairman, Yasser Arafat, promised the Arab Foreign Ministers at the Islamic conference in Cairo,

"The peace accord with Israel is only the first step in an effort to regain lands controlled by Israel, including East Jerusalem. The three million Palestinian refugees outside of Israel will be allowed to return home. Israel must return all territories taken from the '67 war. The agreement we have reached is nothing but a first step. It is the basis for a transitional solution and the broad outline for an ultimate solution that will be based on the ending of the occupation and the total withdrawal from our land...our Holy sites, and our Holy Jerusalem. The most important part of the agreement is not only the withdrawal from Gaza and Jericho, but the recognition of the Palestinian authority and jurisdiction over all the occupied territories."

The basic promise God gave to the Nation of Israel and the Jewish descendants of Abraham is given in Genesis 15:18 with the Covenant God made with Abraham:

"To your descendants I have given this land, from the river of Egypt as far as the great river, the river Euphrates."

All this land was what God promised would eventually be under Jewish control and part of the Nation of Israel. Giving away any of this land violates the Covenant God made with Israel, with the final fulfillment of the boundaries of Israel to come during the Messianic Age.

In regards to specific land in question that the P.L.O. would control, Jericho is predominantly mentioned in the Bible in regards to God's promises to the Jewish successors of Abraham. It is believed that God continued the promise, of inheritance of the land to Moses and Joshua, at the time of the crossing of the Jordan River into the Promised Land. This promise was continued in Joshua 1:3-4 where God spoke to Joshua and said:

"Every place on which the sole of your foot treads, I have given to you, just as I spoke to Moses. From the wilderness and from Lebanon as far as the great river, the river Euphrates as far as the great sea toward the setting of the sun, will be your territory."

The specific right to the city of Jericho was given to the Nation of Israel through God's promise to Joshua in Joshua 6:2 where the Lord said:

"See I have given Jericho into your hand, with its king and the valiant warriors."

The basic principle was laid forth by Joshua in Joshua

6:26, that anyone that fortified the city of Jericho against the Nation of Israel would be cursed with a curse. The Lord made this oath to Joshua after the city of Jericho had been destroyed and all the people killed as per God's instructions to Joshua. Joshua 6:26 gives the oath that Joshua and the Nation of Israel made.

"Joshua made them take an oath at that time, saying, **'Cursed before the Lord is the man who rises up and builds the city Jericho; with the loss of his firstborn he shall lay his foundation, and with the loss of his youngest son he shall set up its gates.'"**

We see an example of the fulfillment of this oath in I Kings 16:34 where Hiel fortified Jericho, and with its foundation he lost his firstborn son, Abiram, and with it's gates, he lost his youngest son, Segub, which the Bible says was according to the Word of the Lord which was spoken by Joshua the son of Nun.

Prime Minister Rabin, as a Bible believing Christian, my face turned red with embarrassment when President Clinton said:

"The sound we heard today, once again as in ancient Jericho, was of trumpets toppling walls, the walls of anger and suspicion between Israeli and Palestinian, between Arab and Jew. This time, praise God, the trumpets herald not the destruction of that city, but its new beginning."

President Clinton praised God that the "trumpets herald not the destruction of Jericho but its new beginning." The walls of Jericho fell by a mighty act of God *because of a glorious miracle. To mock that miracle, or to compare that miracle with what is happening with Jericho today, is an embarrassment to all Bible believing Christians.*

It is quite obvious that with autonomy given to the P.L.O. and the Palestinian people of Jericho, that the city will once again be fortified with its own police force and with heavy security if Yasser Arafat establishes his temporary home and headquarters in that city. The curse of God will descend upon anyone who does this.

While the actual city of Jericho lies within the boundaries of the land originally given to the tribe of Benjamin, the area of Judah and Judea are, without question, lands promised by God Almighty to the Jewish people. This land cannot be devoid of Jewish control and Jewish settlement at that time when God, through the Messiah, defends the Nation of Israel in its time of greatest danger.

Zechariah Chapter 12 and 14 indicate that the last battle of the world will center around Jerusalem and that the Lord will stand on the Mount of Olives to defend the inhabitants of Jerusalem. God specifically states that He will watch over the house of Judah and that the inhabitants of Judah will be saved first before the inhabitants of Jerusalem in this great carnage so that the inhabitants of Jerusalem will not be magnified above Judah. Therefore, it is absolutely imperative that before the coming of the Messianic age and the deliverance of the Nation of Israel through the Messiah, that the ancient boundaries of Judah be under control of the Jewish people, and not under Arafat and the P.L.O. terrorist organization.

While he was here in America, Arafat arrogantly boasted that his P.L.O. flag would fly over Jerusalem, and all aspects of U.N. resolution 242 and 338 must be implemented as a basis for peace.

Mr. Prime Minister, please be kind enough to tell me what the basis is for allowing this terrorist to enter the global community as a world diplomat, serving as head of the 20th Arab state. That will be paramount to the P.L.O. serving as dictators over another hostile Arab state, carved out of the back of the Bible Lands, with its headquarters to be in the very door that God Almighty told Joshua would be the entrance to the Promised Land…Jericho.

Surely, you recognize that the Holy Land is the home not only of the Muslim, and the Jewish faiths, but also the Christian faith. We evangelicals have been strong, courageous and uncompromising supporters of your land.

Mr. Prime Minister, your credentials as a famous General and Chief of Staff are extremely commendable. Please enlighten us on why you would trust Yasser Arafat. Did the Arab world rush to give up its territory when six million Jews died in the Holocaust? No, it was the Jewish people themselves who sacrificed and suffered so that the prophecies could be fulfilled and your beloved people could have a homeland.

It is not the fault of Israel that the Palestinians have had difficulty in Gaza. It is the fault of many current, rich, Arab dictators, who refuse to give a crumb of bread, or a small piece of their vast lands to establish a Palestinian state, but would rather slip a knife in the back of their Arab brothers who attempt to build any bridges based upon mutual respect with your beloved land. Prime Minister Rabin, why the great change in Israel's policy?

We love you and your beloved country more than words can tell, and pray for Israel daily. Mr. Prime Minister, when does a pig have enough to eat? Will Jericho and Gaza satisfy his appetite? How could that be possible when he is already boasting about having East Jerusalem and much more?

What is the basis for faith in an Islamic religion, which has done everything in its power to boycott and unmercifully eliminate the Jewish people? Why did the Jewish people leave all of the 19 Arab states? It surely wasn't because they were treated well. On the contrary, they were hung, burned alive and tortured unmercifully. For what? For being Jewish. Will it be any different in the 20th Arab state under a terrorist leader? Why give the P.L.O. a state when history records that the Palestinians are Jordanians. Seventy percent of all Palestinians carry Jordanian passports. Even if Arafat was a moderate, is it possible that the P.L.O. terrorist organization will improve after Arafat is gone? And, can you really believe that Arafat will survive if he becomes a moderate? Sadat *did not.*

History records that the Arab nations have always run their countries off the bullet not the ballot. As you well know, this feud has gone on for 3,000 years...since the days of Ishmael and Isaac. It is much bigger than a handshake and political speeches.

We evangelicals have no hatred in our hearts toward the Arab people. We love them and pray for them. But we have no respect for an unrepentant terrorist who wants to deceive America and the nations of the world. There will be a man born in days to come who will be like Yasser Arafat, but a thousand times worse. In your Jewish Bible, he is prophesied in the Book of Daniel, Chapter 8:23-25:

"And in the latter time of their kingdom, when the transgressors are come to the full, a king of fierce countenance, and understanding dark sentences, shall stand up. And his power shall be mighty, but not by his power: and he shall destroy wonderfully, and shall prosper, and practice, and shall destroy the mighty and the holy people. And through his policy also he shall cause craft to prosper in his hand; and he shall magnify himself in his heart, and by peace shall destroy many: he shall also stand up against the Prince of princes; but he shall be broken without hand."

Mr. Prime Minister, this prophecy describes a false messiah who will rise up promising peace to the world, and use economic leverage to manipulate the world into that peace. Arafat is a perfect forerunner of that which is to come. The spirit in which Arafat is being influenced by is described in the Book of Revelation 12:9:

"And the great dragon was cast out, that old serpent, called the Devil, and Satan, which deceiveth the whole world: he was cast out into the earth, and his angels were cast out with him" (KJV).

Our former Speaker of the House, Jim Wright and I talked about this matter. Jim Wright explained that he had met with Sadat in Cairo, had flown to Jerusalem to talk to Begin and was in the Knesset when Sadat made his famous speech. I asked Jim Wright, "How much do you know about Arafat? Have you ever met him?" He answered, "No, but he is a charming fellow, wouldn't you agree?" I told my friend, Jim Wright, "I am sure many thought Hitler was a charming fellow, too."

I had a similar conversation with Rev. Jesse Jackson. Rev. Jackson said to me, "This is a wonderful day. It is the beginning of peace. Israel must recognize the golden rule."

I told Rev. Jackson, "**We live in a day when those who have the gold make the rule on the short term. On the long term, man proposes, but God disposes.** God will indeed have the last word when it comes to the Bible Lands and prophecy."

Prime Minister Rabin, we as Bible believing Christians are loyal allies and friends of your beloved land. We have not been consulted concerning the decisions that are being made. Our opinion has not been asked. Are you not *interested in our opinions? If you are, I can tell you, specifically, that evangelicals do not believe that God breaks His promises...or that the Bible is negotiable.*

I was asked by Prime Minister Shamir's Senior Advisor, Dr. Reuben Hecht, if I would speak up for Israel at the 43rd General Assembly of the United Nations at Geneva when your Ambassador and Foreign Minister held their specially convened conference. I told him I would be delighted to do so. I boldly expressed the same view that I am expressing in this letter. Your Foreign Minister made a statement saying:

"No one can be sure of what the Bible says concerning our land, in that we do not determine our foreign policy by the Bible, nor do we know for sure what God says."

There was quite an uproar in Israel over this as I am sure you are aware because of the fact that this was broadcast live to the nation. The truth is that you must determine your foreign policy, and all policies, by the Bible. Your history records leaders upon whom God put His hand, and leaders from whom God removed His hand. David was a man after God's own heart, because he loved God's Word, and he attempted to humble himself...even when he made mistakes. God blessed him. But Saul was rejected by God and cursed. The people in the land experienced a terrible curse because of their disobedience.

We have no intention of seeing the Holy sites that we love so dearly being desecrated as toilets as they were before 1967. How hypocritical for the community of nations to demand that Israel trade land for peace! We did not do it in America with Mexico, nor did we do it with the American Indians. We told the American Indians that they could live in America, but they would have to abide by our rules. What has made our nation great is mutual respect…not trading land for peace.

Can you imagine a Mexican or an Indian terrorist being invited to the White House and applauded by the world community if he proclaimed Washington, D.C., as his capital and had killed, proportionately, the number of people the P.L.O. have killed, over the years, in your land?

Please explain to me, Mr. Prime Minister, so I can communicate it to the evangelical community of America, what the reason is for this festival of hypocrisy and theater of the absurd that I witnessed in Washington, D.C. Is it economic blackmail or is it just a genuine willingness to want peace so desperately that you are willing to take such an enormous risk?

Tom Foley, the Speaker of the House, when asked if he would permit Arafat, in the future, to address the Congress and the Senate in a joint session, he said:

"Seven days ago, I would have said unequivocally, no. But after seeing Arafat today, I would say that it would be highly probable."

Prime Minister Rabin, what in the world did Arafat do to be granted amnesty for all of his acts of butchery? Can you imagine an American doing what Arafat has done in America, slaughtering innocent civilians, hijack-

ing planes, committing unbelievable atrocities, and then the President of the United States throwing him a multi-million dollar party in the White House promising to raise him over $7 billion? Why, the President would be impeached within 24 hours for attempting to conduct himself in such a way.

I could not believe it when I saw many Senators and Congressmen, that I highly respect, standing in line, as if they were at a carnival, attempting to get Yasser Arafat's autograph. If I have ever seen a gathering of the most powerful leaders of the world totally deceived by one man, I saw it that day. As an American, and on behalf of our leaders who are more concerned about political expediency and the history books than they are about human lives, I humbly ask your forgiveness for the embarrassing position in which you were placed.

How in the world can a smile and a handshake be the basis for mutual respect? God only knows how many individuals received a smile and a handshake from Hitler before they were shot in the head.

*How much land, Mr. Prime Minister, can Israel be forced to give up before the security of your beloved nation is jeopardized? At the present moment, **your early warning time is zero.***

How can Israel, whose foundation is based upon God and the Bible and a desire to preserve a homeland for the Jewish people, hope to live in peace with a people whose allegiance is to Allah and whose life is Islam...who are devoted, fanatically, to their own religion, striving to raise the banner of Islam over every inch of Palestine?

In the Islamic religion, "Muslims are required to make war on the Jewish 'infidels' and all others who reject Islam, because this is just punishment. The Islamic Resistance Movement must aspire to the realization of Allah's promises, no matter how long it takes."

The Prophet Allah…has said: "The day of judgment will not come until Muslims fight and kill the Jews."

Mr. Prime Minister, the Arab population in the Middle East is 500 times your size, and their armies outnumber you thirteen-to-one. Their combined air force is three times larger than yours, and they have even a greater advantage in the number of tanks. They need more land like they need a hole in their head. The Arabs have plenty of land to give away, and plenty of money to establish a Palestinian state.

Salman Rushdie still fears for his life because of simply writing the book, Satanic Verses. In the eyes of Islam, he deserves to die. The entire world, all of its journalists and its appeals have not been able to pacify the wrath of Islam fanatics who want to kill Rushdie.

Prime Minister Rabin, in the last 3,000 years, in spite of the signing of 5,721 major peace treaties, there have only been 268 years of peace. The Arab world is still in a state of war against your great nation. They are still boycotting the land of Israel. America still refuses to recognize Jerusalem as your capital and calls your Bible

Land territories occupied.

"Make war upon those who believe not…even if they be people of the book. Make war upon them until idolatry is no more and Allah's religion reigns supreme."

Mr. Prime Minister, as our President forced you to shake Yasser Arafat's hand, the words of the Koran were ringing through my ears. The miracle of the re-birth of Israel in 1948 after 2,536 years of almost uninterrupted foreign subjugation.

The miracle of the restoration of Jerusalem as your Holy capital is indeed a fulfillment of God's promises. God always keeps His promises. That cannot be said for man. The motto of the British 14th Bomber Squad as they flew over Jerusalem in 1917 was "I spread my wings and keep my promise." The British never kept their promise, but God Almighty has. He has been faithful.

When I confronted Yasser Arafat, face-to-face, at the 43rd General Assembly in Geneva, asking him to recognize Jerusalem as your capital and your biblical rights, he went into a rage telling me,

"Shut up. Shut up. Shut up." He asked, "What must I do to make you shut up? Strip tease for you? It would be absurd."

Mr. Prime Minister, I have no intention of shutting up. I believe the Bible, and I, along with Bible believing evangelicals, will courageously stand up for your biblical, historical and humanitarian rights…in spite of weak-kneed politicians or the liberal press.

Prime Minister Rabin, the P.L.O. covenant in Article II denies the possibility of dividing mandatory Palestine into more than one state. Article VI excludes all Jews who arrive in Palestine after 1917 from remaining in the projected Arab Palestine state. Article IX offers armed struggle as the only way to liberate Palestine. Article XIX and XX declares illegal the Balfour Declaration, and the mandate for Palestine, and the 1947 U.N. decision to petition Palestine and establish the state of Israel and which determines the Jews are members of a religion not a nationality or a nation. I do not need to remind you of Article XXII challenging Zionism.

Mr. Prime Minister, I realize that a great number of the Jewish organizations in America are applauding your meeting with Arafat...as are the World Council of Churches. Both of these organizations have a lot in common. They both reject the Bible as the Word of God.

We evangelicals accept the Bible as non-negotiable. God Almighty exists, and He miraculously gave your beloved people Jericho, how in the world can this same Jericho be given to Arafat as his transitional capital? Has anyone asked God's opinion or even consulted your Eternal Declaration of Independence...the Word of God?

I realize that you do have peace, to some degree, with Egypt because Anwar al-Sadat presented a new type of Islam in which he said,

"No religion in politics. No politics in religion...an ecumenical Islam."

But as you well know, Sadat was not quoting from the Koran. This was a new philosophy that he thought he could sell to the Islamic world, but as we say in Texas, "that dog won't hunt." His Muslim brothers assassinated Sadat for being what they considered a traitor to their cause.

I want to remind you of what Yasser Arafat did in 1981 at the Islamic conference in Mecca when he pressed for a swearing of a collective oath by Muslim delegation heads binding them to afford all means to liberate Jerusalem. This time, however, Saudi King Khalid managed to dissuade him. According to Saudi Foreign Minister, Saud al-Faysal,

"There was a proposal on the liberation of Jerusalem at the opening session of the Islamic conference in the Mecca Mosque. King Khalid asserted to the P.L.O. leader that the meeting of Muslims near the Ka-ba in the house of God, in a conference designated as the Palestinian and Jerusalem conference is already a binding pledge to liberate Holy Jerusalem... 'I believe that the whole conference represents a pledge by Muslims to liberate Jerusalem."

Has anything really changed in the minds of the Arab leaders of the Middle East?

In 1970, Jordan was virtually overthrown by Yasser Arafat because of his terrorist activities. It was your own nation that saved Jordan from this maniac. Why in the world would you want to sandwich him between the Holy City of Jerusalem and Jordan?

The Arab world wants Jerusalem. They have their own version of "next year in Jerusalem," and it is not based upon the desire to pray for the return of the Messiah, but to drive your beloved people out of the land.

But God keeps His promises, and the Word of God proclaims...

"I will restore the captivity of my people, Israel, and they will rebuild the ruined cities and live in them. They will also plant vineyards and drink their wine, and make gardens, and eat their fruit. I will also plant them in the land, and they will not again be rooted out from their land...which I have given them...says the Lord your God" (Jeremiah 29:4-10).

Mr. Prime Minister, from the old border, the pre-1967 border, the distance is nine miles, or fifteen kilometers. This is the distance between Kennedy Airport and Queens in New York. From the Jordan River or the Jordanian territory that is east of the Jordan River to Jerusalem...is six minutes. This is with an F5G with a full load of bombs at a low altitude. As a military General, you have to know that in strictly military terms, you have about four minutes of early warning time. Four minutes of early warning time, in practical terms, means zero warning time.

What guarantee do you have that Russia will not ultimately move in the direction of your land in the future? Your Jewish Bible predicts in Ezekiel 38, by the prophet Ezekiel, that indeed she will. And by the way, Mr.

Prime Minister, two-thirds of the prophecies of your Jewish prophets have already been fulfilled concerning your land. God does keep His promises. General George Keegan, a former head of the U.S. Air Force, mentioned to me in the past that if the West Bank were to fall into Arafat's hands, and two brigades of well-equipped Soviet divisions were introduced into the West Bank, in one night, Israel would cease to exist. I don't believe it will cease to exist because the Bible prophesies a battle called the Battle of Armageddon. But God forbid that the winds of that battle have to blow prematurely because of mistakes made by man...because of a world that wants Israel to give up its territory and lose the security of its nation.

President Clinton referred to the Arab and Palestinian children and said that this decision needed to be made for their safety. What will the Soviet Union be like ten or twenty years from now? High-level Soviet Generals, with whom I have met, have told me that there will ultimately be a revolution and it will be worse than before. If indeed that is the case, could your decision be forcing the children of Israel into a premature Armageddon?

Prime Minister Rabin, when I founded the Prayer Breakfast in honor of Israel in conjunction with the National Religious Broadcasters, I gave a speech, which is in the Congressional Record.

Mr. Prime Minister, the land of Palestine belongs to the Jewish people. Millions of evangelicals signed this proclamation. I appeal to you to read Psalm 83:3-5...espe-

cially these words…

"Those who hate thee have exalted themselves. They make shrewd plans against thy people and conspire together against thy treasured ones. They have said come let us wipe them out as a nation. Let the name of Israel be remembered no more. They have conspired together with one mind against thee to make a covenant."

The Chief Rabbi of Jerusalem met with Harry Truman in the White House concerning the re-establishment of your state. He said,

"President Truman, God put you in your mother's womb to bring about the re-birth of Israel after 2,000 years."

President Truman had the courage to stand up and acknowledge Israel's biblical rights. As amazing as it might sound, the Soviets did also.

Please Mr. Prime Minister, God did not put you in your mother's womb to bring about the destruction of Israel. The Word of God declares in Isaiah 62:6-7…

"I have set watchmen upon the walls O Jerusalem which shall never hold their peace…day or night. He that make mention of the Lord keep not silent. Give him no rest until he make Jerusalem a praise in the earth. Comfort ye. Comfort ye my people, saith your God."

The Bible also says…

"When they shall cry peace and safety, then shall come sudden destruction upon them as travail upon a woman with child."

Jerusalem is facing its greatest threat in its 3,000-year history.

Mr. Prime Minister, call the people of the Book to humble themselves and fast and pray on these your Holy days. God is able to do what no man can do. He has done it before for your beloved land. Let me quote from II Chronicles 7:14:

"If my people, which are called by my name, shall humble themselves, and pray, and seek my face, and turn from their wicked ways; then will I hear from heaven, and will forgive their sin, and will heal their land."

I humbly appeal to you to call your nation to humble themselves, fast and pray based upon II Chronicles 7:14 that the God of Heaven will hear and answer your prayers. More than anything else, Israel needs a revival…a spiritual rebirth. That spiritual rebirth, indeed, will bring God's blessings and favor.

You are giving up everything. Yasser Arafat, and his P.L.O. terrorist organization, is giving up nothing. If that is the basis for a marriage, then Yasser Arafat will become delighted to be married to your beloved land.

Mr. Prime Minister, always remember…when you dance with a gorilla, the dance isn't over with until the gorilla says so.

With sincere prayers for the peace of Jerusalem and the land of Israel, above all,

Michael David Evans"

Why should Christians support Israel? Because it is God's will to do so! It is impossible to believe the Bible, and not know that.

The Jerusalem
Prayer Team

"Pray for the peace of Jerusalem…" (Psalm 122:6).

After 61 days of fasting and prayer, God spoke the vision for the Jerusalem Prayer Team in my heart. This was to be God's dream and God's team. After I heard from heaven, I flew to Jerusalem to meet with Mayor Ehud Olmert to share the vision of the Jerusalem Prayer Team. He was greatly touched, and flew to Dallas in June 2002 to inaugurate this prayer movement. Dr. Franklin Graham, Dr. Jerry Falwell, Prime Minister Benjamin Netanyahu, Representative Dick Armey, and Governor Rick Perry were some of those who participated either by letter or video.

Christians from all over America have joined the Jerusalem Prayer Team. Many are household names, i.e., Rev. Tommy Tenney, Dr. Pat Robertson, Coach Bill McCartney, Dr. Tim LaHaye, Dr. John Maxwell, Mr. Pat Boone, Dr. David Clark, Dr. Michael Little, Ms. Kay Arthur, and others.

During the inaugural event, Mayor Ehud Olmert said:

"I wish to thank you on behalf of the people of Jerusalem for your support, for your care, for your love, for your friendship, for your generosity. I will go back... to Jerusalem, and I will tell the people of Jerusalem that we have established here in Dallas something that will spread across America, and later across the world...the Jerusalem Prayer Summits...the Jerusalem Prayer Team...that I have the honor to inaugurate today. I promised it to my friend, Mike Evans, that I would join him in going from one congregation to the other, from one community to the other to participate in the Jerusalem Prayer Summits. And we will talk, and we will approach people, and we will share with them the responsibility and the love that Christians and Jews have together for the destiny of Jerusalem. For the future of Jerusalem, for the love of God for this city, for the love of God for all of us, thank you, thank you from Jerusalem. God bless all of you!"

Franklin Graham said in a letter (read at the inaugural Prayer Summit): *"...I certainly wish you and all those participating God's blessing and that God will use this to help strengthen the Jewish people. We have all been dismayed at how much positive media attention these fanatic Muslims are getting in this country and we certainly pray for the peace of Jerusalem."*

The vision of the Jerusalem Prayer Team is to

have ten million intercessors praying daily for national revival according to 2 Chronicles 7:14 as prophesied by King David's son, Solomon. Also pray the prayer of King David who declared: "*Pray for the peace of Jerusalem; they shall prosper that love thee.*" Praying for the peace of Jerusalem is not praying for stones or dirt. They don't weep or bleed. It is praying for God's protection over the lives of the citizens of Jerusalem. It is praying for revival. It is praying for God's grace to be poured out.

Mother Teresa was one of the first people to tell me she would pray daily for the Peace of Jerusalem in Rome according to Psalm 122:6. She said to me, "*Love is not something you say, it's something you do.*" I believe that with all my heart. That is why I am appealing to you to join me in seeing what King David saw…what Solomon saw…and what our beloved Lord saw as they prayed in Jerusalem. Each experienced the power of God in Jerusalem—God's glory filled the house where they stood!

We are asking for ten million Christians to join the Jerusalem Prayer Team, and are asking 100,000 churches to begin praying weekly during their Sunday services for the peace of Jerusalem.

Would you become a Jerusalem Prayer Team member, and would you encourage others to do so? If you will pray daily, if you will be a part of the Lord's answering this prayer, and a part of touching the destiny of the City of David, then contact me at The Jerusalem Prayer Team, P. O. Box 30000, Phoenix, AZ 85046.